MASTERING
MONEY

MASTERING
MONEY

HOW TO BEAT DEBT, BUILD WEALTH, AND BE PREPARED FOR ANY FINANCIAL CRISIS

NORM CHAMP

NEW YORK   CHICAGO   SAN FRANCISCO   ATHENS
LONDON   MADRID   MEXICO CITY   MILAN
NEW DELHI   SINGAPORE   SYDNEY   TORONTO

1 2 3 4 5 6 7 8 9   LCR   24 23 22 21 20 19

ISBN   978-1-260-45253-2
MHID   1-260-45253-0

e-ISBN   978-1-260-45254-9
e-MHID   1-260-45254-9

Library of Congress Cataloging-in-Publication Data

Names: Champ, Norm, author.
Title: Mastering money : how to beat debt, build wealth, and be prepared for any financial crisis / Norm Champ.
Description: New York : McGraw-Hill, [2020] | Includes bibliographical references and index.
Identifiers: LCCN 2019028384 (print) | LCCN 2019028383 (ebook) | ISBN 9781260452532 (hardcover) | ISBN 9781260452549 (ebook)
Subjects: LCSH: Finance, Personal—United States. | Debt—United States.
Classification: LCC HG181 .C49 2020 (ebook) | LCC HG181 (print) | DDC 332.02400973—dc23
LC record available at https://lccn.loc.gov/2019028384

This publication is designed to provide accurate and authoritative information in regard to the subject matter covered. It is sold with the understanding that neither the author nor the publisher is engaged in rendering legal, accounting, securities trading, or other professional services. If legal advice or other expert assistance is required, the services of a competent professional person should be sought.

—From a Declaration of Principles Jointly Adopted by a
Committee of the American Bar Association
and a Committee of Publishers and Associations

*This book is dedicated to everyone
who wants to be a net worth warrior*

PART 1
Take Hold of the Spending Governor

PART 2
Increase Inflow

PART 3
Investing for the Future

I thank my wife, Sally, and our four wonderful children for putting up with my various projects. They are the most important people in my life.

I also would like to thank all of the people who have urged me forward on this book. I have been so encouraged by how many people have shown a real interest in improving financial literacy for all. Thank you to Donya Dickerson at McGraw-Hill, publisher of my first book, *Going Public*, for seeing the possibilities in a second book.

My editor, Herb Schaffner, is my invaluable companion on this journey through two books.

Finally, to all of my friends, colleagues, and clients—a heartfelt thank you for your friendship and support. None of it happens without you.

Taking Back Financial Control

I love money. I love everything about it. I bought some pretty good stuff. Got me a $300 pair of socks. Got a fur sink. An electric dog polisher. A gasoline powered turtleneck sweater. And, of course, I bought some dumb stuff, too.

—STEVE MARTIN

I did not write this book to sell you anything. I don't have wealth-building seminars, tapes, courses, or consulting to tout. I am a lawyer at a major law firm and am not looking for a second career as a financial guru. I decided to write *Mastering Money* after working for five years at the U.S. Securities and Exchange Commission (SEC) in Washington, right after the crash of the 2008 Great Recession. What I witnessed during that time—bureaucratic mismanagement, wasted taxpayer money, the hidden taxation effect of bad policies and grandiose regulations, the devastating impact of small-time fraudsters on the savings of ordinary people, and the vulnerability of all working Americans to the next economic crisis—confirmed my worries that ordinary families are facing a crisis of financial illiteracy and instability. One major reason: the federal government and in many cases our K–12 school system are not making financial literacy a priority. What's worse, many financial rules and regulations are written to serve partisan or industry interests, not the public interest. I wrote this book because I saw that this situation must change.

A 2015 survey from the National Foundation for Credit Counseling found that 4 in 10 adults gave themselves a grade of C, D, or F on their finance knowledge. One-third hadn't saved anything for retirement, another third had no savings, and 6 in 10 did not have a budget. John Pelletier, executive director of the Center for Financial Literacy at Champlain College, said of the survey, "Such negative financial outcomes and low levels of consumer knowledge and confidence make it crystal clear that financial literacy in America should be a national priority."[1]

I've witnessed the results of this knowledge gap. From Bernie Madoff's victims to the people waiting in line at the pro bono legal aid truck where I volunteer, I have seen many good people with good intentions living on the brink. They're getting irresponsible advice, the wrong signals from society, bad incentives from their government, and little financial literacy training in our schools. They're living in fear because of financial problems, and despite it all, they want to find a way to right their ship. They want to recapture their piece of the American Dream again.

And they can. And you can. Starting today.

I've been in the front lines at the SEC trying to stop the devastating effects of fraud and investor scams. I've studied how the government isn't looking out for you—whether it is the legal scam of the lottery or the cheap money printed by the Federal Reserve after the 2008 crisis. The government wants us to be a nation of bored shoppers, not savers. For too long, the United States has "normalized living beyond one's means," wrote Sheldon Garon, Nissan Professor of History and East Asian Studies at Princeton University, who took a scholarly interest in the history of saving and consumer finance. "For the last several decades, America has been preoccupied with democratizing credit. Surely, the time has come to democratize saving. It should be as easy for any American to open a savings account as it is to get a credit card."[2]

It's time for us to take our financial destiny back into our own hands.

I wrote this book because I wanted to help you learn the fundamentals of getting your finances in order and beginning to invest in the future. The 1-2-3 process I will show is a reliable and time-tested approach to peace of mind and financial freedom. But only you can blaze this path to your future.

The basics of mastering money are not complicated, but our society has buried them for so long they've become secrets.

Self-made people who are financially secure mastered money by accepting a simple, hard truth, the bottom line to the bottom line: you must take charge of building your own balance sheet. Earned income needs to exceed expenses, including debt. When you run a positive balance, you can save and increase your balance sheet. Your savings are your safety net and your shield. Unlike a financed car or a credit card, no one can take away money you save.

We're a nation of immigrants and pioneers, enriched by the honest struggle of those who overcame slavery, poverty, and all manner of the toughest odds. At our best, we are a nation that made a better life through work and thrift to advance our children and grandchildren to a stronger place. We did this through education, community, hard work, and the stable neighborhoods that flourished when people could honestly afford to buy or rent their homes and apartments with sound money. In America, every generation is enriched by the fruits of entrepreneurs who achieved success through hard work and a desire to extend the American Dream to the next generation.

Twentieth-century Americans built the world's greatest job-creating democracy. They didn't do it with high-interest credit cards and handouts or lottery tickets—or by scraping by on benefit checks they didn't need. They worked, they saved, they made smart investments, and they practiced thrift. They made weekly deposits in community banks or savings and loans, back when these were called *thrift institutions*. After the Great Depression, our government wisely protected bank savings accounts and made sure that banks had the reserves to guarantee their customers' life savings.

But our best days are not necessarily behind us. The upside of where we are now is that despite all the controversy, all the headlines, all the bad news, our current economy continues to offer far more job opportunities and sound investing options than our grandparents would have dreamed of.

Financial peace of mind is closer than you think.

MONEY MISTAKES START IN CHILDHOOD

When my siblings and I were growing up in Missouri, we lived like a family with financial security. I didn't worry about money and was able to attend college without debt, which made a significant positive difference in my fortunes. Under the surface, though, chaos brewed.

I suppose some would say my ambition and work ethic are hallmarks of the ACOA (adult child of an alcoholic) personality, and if so, I came by them honestly. My past gives me a powerful radar for picking up on the national addiction to debt and spending in our society.

Ultimately, it would take years for me to understand all the ways my family influenced my behavior and how it resulted in money mistakes. The process was among the most stressful years of my life, but it was my education in the tragic consequences of ignoring financial reality.

Because I grew up in financial chaos, I became motivated to get my finances in order early. I understand that life is messy, and families face many challenges in getting control of their finances. An essential step in mastering your money is to assess your behaviors and identify how your past influenced them so that you can use this awareness to change. I will provide a resource for these assessments at the end of this chapter.

If you have experienced difficulties growing up, they can have lasting effects on your money behavior and career. People who have adverse childhood experiences are significantly more likely to report having financial stress, poor work performance, drug and alcohol abuse, a wide range of health problems, and poor academic achievement, according to a study by Fellitti, Anda, and Nordenberg published in the *American Journal of Preventative Medicine*.[3]

The point is: know thyself.

Each of you will have your own entirely unique journey toward mastering money. You will have challenges that no one else will encounter. I learned from my trials and experiences. *I encourage you to assess your attitudes, behaviors, and life experiences that have influenced your current financial life and your opinions about money.* Then use the fundamental principles taught in this book, depending on your circumstances.

Many different experts and publications put forward financial assessment tools. I recommend browsing the internet and looking for a few quality assessments that speak to you. If you want an objective, nonbiased approach, check out the tests developed by Rutgers' Agricultural Experiment Station along with other academic and nonprofit experts. The quizzes aren't slanted toward a particular self-interest or to promote a particular product. Rutgers' land-use agency has a 225-year-old public education mission. The instruments cover *financial fitness, identity theft risk assessment, investment risk tolerance, personal resiliency,* and *wise credit.* They can be found at https://njaes.rutgers.edu/money/assessment-tools/. I've taken a look at them myself, and they are carefully done!

So your assignment is to spend a few hours taking these various assessments and then reviewing the results. I trust that you will never regret a moment of learning how your experiences have shaped—often at an unconscious level—your beliefs about money and work.

TAKE HOLD OF THE SPENDING GOVERNOR

The title of this part isn't telling you to grab your state's elected governor on the rope line. The state police bodyguards wouldn't like that. The word *governor* also refers to a device that measures and regulates the speed of an engine. Most engines now have an automatic governor that limits the amount of gas that the engine can take so that it does not overheat in the case of a lawnmower or scooter or in the case of an automobile exceed a preset maximum speed limit. In the early days of the automobile, the driver could directly manage the speed of the car by manually shifting the governor to a preset speed. Too many Americans have lost their inner governor when it comes to spending, particularly click-and-buy spending online. Because Amazon isn't going to send you an alert if you exceed some pre-agreed level of spending (not a bad idea)—and I'm not picking on Amazon; this applies to the whole consumer credit economy—we have to get our minds and hands on the governor to our impulsive spending engine.

Think Before You Click

Commercialism is more a mirror than a lamp. In demonizing it, in seeing ourselves as helpless and innocent victims of its overpowering force…we reveal far more about our own eagerness to be passive in the face of complexity than about the thing itself.
—JAMES TWITCHELL, PROFESSOR OF ENGLISH, UNIVERSITY OF FLORIDA[1]

THE CONSUMER MADHOUSE

Human beings must exchange money for food, shelter, and clothing to survive. Beyond that, we innately enjoy owning things that can provide us with satisfaction, pleasure and, of course, entertainment. We fervently, urgently enjoy getting those things we desire. We even—and I mean this in the nicest way, really—lose our minds a little bit when we are in hot pursuit. Neuroscientists have actually mapped how we're programmed from our evolutionary past to get things we want *pronto* and not to "waste time" considering the better outcome that might be achieved by waiting.[2]

We modern-day humans must fight hard and smart to focus on our fiscal health. Every type of marketplace we enter—from farmers' markets to shopping malls to online click-and-buy—presents a superabundance of choices, marketed with clever schemes designed to work on our psychosocial trigger points. The online abundance we experience today simply did not exist 100 years ago. It has been building steadily in my lifetime, from what I have seen, and we've reached a peak. In the online marketplace, scientists have determined our emotional responses to the attractive presentation of merchandise, and "calm, friendly, knowledgeable" ad copy is even quicker to trigger impulse spending than are regular retail shops.[3] We know that many of these digital ads, replete with video and graphics, present delightful consumer experiences and promises of endless adventures, posing unprecedented challenges to people's ability to focus on long-term financial security.

"We are wired, for now, to be impulsive," said Dr. Phil Harris in describing a 2017 study he did on the topic of spending habits.[4] Harris found that test subjects were better able to control their spending urges after looking at digitally aged photos of themselves and visualizing their lives 20 years on. Perhaps there's a quick tip in that methodology: try thinking about gray hair and crows' feet the next time you are browsing online. It *could* help, I suppose. But in this chapter I will suggest many more defined and strategic ways to build self-control over spending.

Only 40 or 50 years ago—less than a lifetime—people had no choice but to save for what they wanted before they could buy it. Stashing away money weekly for a vacation or putting it in a Christmas Club bank account meant that people had time to think about how much they wanted to spend—or didn't—on a particular purchase. It was part of the culture back then to care about every dollar.

I'm certainly not proselytizing against the joys of spontaneous shopping. I take pleasure in buying well-made clothes, having a celebratory dinner out with family, and buying gifts for my kids on their birthdays. I relish acquiring a great suit for work or a couple of pairs of snazzy shorts when I visit the beach. But I have also devoted my attention for many years to learning how not to overspend and how to live within my family's means. About those things, I do proselytize a little, especially at home. I work with my kids so that they will grasp how to be prudent with their own money as they achieve adulthood. I believe that a fundamental component of true adulthood is the ability to be self-sufficient.

When I say self-sufficient, I'm not talking about being Captain Fantastic, teaching my kids how to live off the land (Viggo Mortensen starred in the movie, if you haven't seen it), but I want them to appreciate the value of what they have and how to resist the psychology of impulse spending. We can all be so easily parted from our money in this twenty-first-century consumer madhouse. It really is a jungle out there in many respects, a jungle thick with exotic market schemes that prey on our most basic human instincts.

In this chapter I will show you how we get manipulated into excessive spending and recount the techniques you need to know to avoid being ripped off. Out-of-control consumerism isn't just an issue for shopaholics anymore. In the current realm of click-and-get online shopping, smartphone apps, and so on, you can spend so quickly that automatic renewals and monthly subscriptions are picking your pocket before you realize what's happening. There's no governor. Marketers know how to make those "cancel your subscription prompts" invisible and how difficult it can be for us to turn off what's been switched on in our brains—and our bank accounts. Home mortgages, car loans, and notoriously unthrifty and risky borrowing behaviors such as taking out a home equity line of credit (HELOC) or using a second mortgage to redo your kitchen or put in a swimming pool will be addressed in Chapter 4.

CHECK OUT ANY TIME YOU LIKE

Even in simpler times, back when everyone's consciousness was not pecked at every second by a million provocations and distractions emanating from phone and computer screens, it was easy to get people salivating over the latest new product with a well-placed ad in the newspaper or on TV. Even rural American settlers in the late nineteenth century could be seduced by the offerings of the Sears catalog delivered by the U.S. Post Office horse and buggy. People can be conveniently lulled into forgetting about fees and monthly commitments when they dream about bringing those products home. It has always been easy to distract us humans with something pretty or sexy, and it always will be. Marketing schemes aimed at taking advantage of this tendency are inevitably successful at grabbing bits and chunks of our money.

Back in the 1990s, it was the siren song of music (and a "join-the-club" hook) that first lured so many young people, including me, into the land of recurring fees and obligations that seemed too difficult to remember to cancel. You thought you'd struck musical gold when you scored a pile of tapes or CDs for a penny—simply for agreeing to buy a few more at the regular price over time. It was the deal of a (youngish) lifetime. Alas, those "regular price" CDs turned out to be much more expensive than the average retail store price, even if that wasn't clear in the promotional material. And many of us music lovers eventually came to feel that music club membership bore a certain resemblance to The Eagles' "Hotel California," where you wander right on in but never leave. Technically, you could leave, of course, but it was kind of a bureaucratic hassle. More to the point, you'd have to pay up on all the more-than-regular-price albums you'd agreed to buy when you became a club member. So, what the heck, why not let it slide for another month? Oops.

Okay, one more month.

Oops, etc., etc.[5]

LONG-PLAYING SCHEME

That was the mentality marketing agents keyed into when the Columbia record label began selling vinyl records via mail order way back in 1955 and, as formats morphed over the years, eight-tracks, cassettes, and then CDs by the 1980s. The essence of the subscription deal Columbia House offered never changed through the decades: get a bunch of albums for 1 cent, and agree to buy a few more at regular prices over time. As teenagers have been wont to say through the ages, *"Everyone's* doing it!" It was practically irresistible to music lovers on tight budgets (or parental allowances) who craved a personal collection. For those residing at the far end of one of John Denver's "Country Roads," or lacking a store they could walk to, Columbia House membership presented a convenient option.

The problem that developed for many customers, though, was that they failed to take the option of saying "no"—or at least "no more"—after the original commitment was made. (Note that Columbia House is now dead and moldering like a box of old cassette tapes in a trash pile. But the DNA behind its marketing scheme is still alive and kicking consumers in the pocketbook. So read on, and *caveat emptor*, forevermore.)

Piotr Orlov, a former marketing director for Columbia House, discussed in a National Public Radio (NPR) commentary in 2015 how the company had hornswoggled millions of young people into signing contracts, knowing that many would neglect to cancel. This was the key: if a record club subscriber did nothing, the obligation was still legally binding. Orlov worked at Columbia House in the late 1990s. By then, he said, it had become almost a rite of passage for young people to take their first shot at "ruining their credit rating" by ignoring further notices after getting free music.[6]

Our government regulators are often slow to pick up on rules that need to be enforced—or toughened. But in 2009, the Federal Trade Commission (FTC) did explicitly warn consumers to beware of subscription-based marketing, issuing a special report on the subject. The regulatory commission used a "jargon-y" term, *negative-options marketing*, which it explained this way: "[t]he FTC uses the phrase to refer to transactions in which sellers interpret a customer's failure to take an 'affirmative action'—either to reject an offer or cancel an agreement—as permission to charge them for goods or services. Negative option marketing can pose *serious financial risks to consumers* if appropriate disclosures are not made and consumers are billed for goods or services without their consent" [emphasis added]. Another way of saying this: if you don't opt-out, you're paying up. I will share some good news in Chapter 8: some wise organizations are using *negative option* to encourage tax-protected savings.

In plain English, the message to consumers was (and is) don't subscribe unless you are going to remember to unsubscribe, because companies can hold you liable until you officially do that. You *will* end up paying more than you intended to spend. Like many messages from regulatory agencies that are supposed to be protecting our financial interests, though, it was pretty obscure to the average consumer. And it came late, way late.

By the time the FTC threw down the red flag on the negative-options game, digital media and online marketing had already transformed the global marketplace. The use of negative-option techniques remained as pervasive as ever, though: *"You're a winner!!! FREE $1,000 at Amazon, Walmart, Sam's Club!!!"* in flashing lights, with ringing bells and a trill of triumphant music, followed by the message: "You need only fulfill five of these available offers [in teeny, tiny print] within a limited number of days, and then you will be eligible to win!"

I have to ask, is there anyone reading this today who has *not* ever been declared a winner online? If so, you might actually be the lucky winner in the crowd. You have not been led into temptation or tried to fulfill all the offers within the correct time frame, found yourself obligated to a variety of recurring automatic purchases, and been ensnared just as securely as any music-loving teen ever was in those analog days of yore.

An authoritative report by McKinsey Global Research confirms the obvious: subscriptions are an increasingly common way to buy products and services online.[7] The most popular services are Amazon Subscribe & Save (consumer packaged goods) and Dollar Shave Club (razors). The advent of subscription digital media services—including Netflix, Hulu, Spotify, and Apple Music—helped fuel near-steroidal growth in the e-commerce market. Between 2011 and 2015, subscription e-commerce swelled from $57 million in $2.5 billion. By early 2018, McKinsey Global Research reported that nearly half of consumers surveyed subscribed to an online streaming-media service such as Netflix. McKinsey also found that more than a third of consumers hold *three or more* online subscriptions. The churn rate is high; people get dissatisfied and cancel, but as the market researchers noted, often people just switch to another subscription media service and restart the cycle.

GIVE-AND-GRAB DIGITAL-STYLE

Many online memberships offer a free or highly discounted trial period, followed by automatic billing. This applies to media offerings and also consumer products, such as Dollar Shave Club or Blue Apron meal kits. I enjoy Spotify and Netflix like many of you. However, I try to keep it just to those. Even if you are initially attracted by introductory rates and offers, even when it comes to specialty items that one savors and receives with anticipation each week or month, it's critical to develop *savoir faire* about canceling and "discount bonus items." Sometimes products can appear on your doorstep without being ordered. How difficult is it to return a bottle of fine Italian red wine when you are *already holding it in your hand*? How hard is it to send back a pizza lacking pepperoni when the smell has already got your mouth watering? It takes near superhuman strength. Minnesota Attorney General Lori Swanson, who has an impressive record of consumer advocacy, has produced a helpful guide to this, ahem, borderline fraud. "Under state and federal law," Swanson writes, "recipients of unordered merchandise may keep the goods and are under no obligation to pay for or return them. The recipient may treat the merchandise as an unconditional gift—and may use or dispose of the merchandise as he or she sees fit. The recipient also may refuse to accept delivery. Federal law states that the sender cannot send you a bill or collection notice for unordered merchandise."[8]

So maybe we should talk about building up your strength. Uh-oh. Who would have thought? This turns out to be where many people's best intentions can hit a wall. You want to get physically stronger, so you join a gym and summon mental strength to commit to it. You quite logically assume that you are investing in something that deserves a serious commitment: your health. The postcards that filled your mailbox and come-ons that flooded your screen appealed to you with deals that were easy on the wallet—"as low as $10 a month!"—and they inspired a feeling that the company is on your side in this exercise. The company *wants* you to be fit! Just show up and use its facility for the cost of several cups of coffee and make a healthier person of yourself.

Of course, once inside the gym door, you will inevitably face the hard sell on "offers" to sign up for pricey personal training. The trainer will keep you personally engaged, if you go for it, but that will require a much bigger commitment of your time, not to mention your money. Whether or not you do add the cost of training to your low introductory fee, you may at some point realize that you are not really getting your money's worth from your gym membership. And then a vicious cycle can ensue.

I'll never forget joining a gym in St. Louis one summer when I was home from college. My friend and I signed up and went there to lift weights. Almost instantly a trainer began trying to persuade me to buy a workout belt to brace my back during lifting. While my friend is a guy who can lift serious weight, I don't think I've ever benched more than 120 pounds or so at my peak. In those college days, I had no money for an expensive leather workout belt, so I kept putting the guy off. Although the sales pitch started making me think I did need a belt, I just couldn't afford it. After repeatedly being rebuffed, the aggressive trainer finally looked at me and said, "No belt, no progress!," and stormed away. I never did buy a lifting belt, but I often think back to the line, "No belt, no progress!," when someone is trying to sell me something I don't need.

You will likely feel guilty if you want to quit because it was your choice to join the gym and get fit in the first place. You may very well—and trust me, the marketers are counting on this possibility— dawdle about canceling your membership. After all, it's your own "fault" you have not morphed into The Incredible Hulk or Wonder Woman or managed to shave at least an inch of belly fat. Maybe it is, and maybe it isn't. What I can assure you of absolutely is that you have gotten tangled up in a sophisticated marketing scheme specifically designed to forestall or, at least, delay the day you cancel your membership.

In a *New York Times* "Your Money" column, Planet Fitness was listed as one of the most-canceled subscription memberships of any type. The article used statistics gathered by Trim, a computer app that tracks recurring charges. Trim's data showed that more than 30 percent of those who sign up with Planet Fitness wind up canceling—and that they often get a real workout trying to do it, according to Trim's cofounder Thomas Smyth.[9] He was quoted in the article as saying that his company assesses the cancellation process for health clubs in general to be "particularly noxious." Because it is designed to assist users in canceling unwanted subscriptions, Trim continually updates its information about the requirements to quit each company. Planet Fitness and other fitness clubs usually do not let you cancel online or with a quick text message. No, it may require sending registered mail to the corporate parent to break up with these muscle factories.

WAIT, WHAT ARE THE RULES?

Some subscription services use a sort of shell game to thwart easy cancellation, switching around the procedures so frequently— I am talking about you, Experian—that the process becomes an endurance contest. In the *Times* article mentioned earlier, Smyth described how companies employ basic principles of psychology and behavioral economics to pick pocketbooks. Or get you to pick your own, if you want to put it that way. He said that companies such as Experian rely on people's natural tendency toward inertia and their impatience with "fine print" to get them off track in defending their personal fiscal fitness.

Smyth also cited the example of Gogo, the digital media service that allows users to connect to Wi-Fi in-flight and become a subscriber. "The per-month rate is often not that much more than the per-day or per-flight rate," Smyth said. "So you look at it and say, 'I'm going to be a winner. I'm smarter than these guys!' And then you forget to cancel. For months."

Please do not feel insulted by this observation. You may actually be smarter than the marketers who wind up feeding off your forgetfulness, but you have fallen prey to their tricks. You were not attentive enough, or aggressive enough, to keep your fiscal wits about you.

By the way, should you want to give the Trim app a try—or another one such as Truebill or Prosper Daily—you can do it for free. You must, however, be willing to submit credit and debit login information or else mail in hard copies of your bills so that the app can scan your statements and identify hidden charges. Ron Lieber, the "Your Money" columnist for the *Times*, submitted his own information when investigating Trim. He said that the app found nine monthly fees—not including those for utilities—totaling more than $100 on his accounts. He used Trim to instantly cancel two of them.

WHAT ARE THE STAKES?

At Truebill, a typical user has 11 recurring charges—mostly services that users know about and want, said Truebill founder and chief executive Yahya Mokhtarzada. (Netflix is most common, followed by Spotify, Amazon Prime, AT&T, and GoDaddy.) Among the 17 percent of site users who cancel a membership, however, the average savings is $512 per year.

Perhaps that's peanuts to you. Perhaps you feel that marketing schemes are not real crookery, only small-time scams not warranting a lot of agita. In that case, please consider the following: the exact same mechanisms are at work in major and undeniable scams, the ones you read about in screaming newspaper headlines or see on TV exposés. There is a direct line connecting petty thieving through subscription fees and notorious swindle operations such as the payday loans scandal documented in the recent Netflix series "Dirty Money" (see the second episode on payday loans mogul Scott Tucker, https://www.netflix.com/title/80118100). Tucker, a millionaire racecar driver, was able to rob people of modest means using a predatory payday loan scheme that carried undisclosed fees. Some borrowers wound up owing as much as three times their initial loans, with Tucker's company charging interest rates as high as 700 percent. More than 1.5 million folks were duped into paying these ridiculous charges. They couldn't *all* have been stupid and irresponsible; they were human beings manipulated with common tricks into confusion about the true cost of something they needed (most people who take these loans are in desperate need of money). The documentary recounts how well-meaning, frightened customers were led to believe that they were paying back the loan when they were only paying back additional hidden fees that triggered even more fees.

The unscrupulous Mr. Tucker is now serving a term of 16 years and 8 months in federal prison (plus having to pay a $1.26 billion judgment). His business manager and partner in crime is also in prison and forfeited $49 million. The AMG Services company they ran was exposed by federal prosecutors in open court as having lied to consumers and regulators about where it was based and having falsely claimed it was run by a Native American tribe. This only occurred after enough alarmed customers complained to state regulators and consumer protection groups that the feds finally got involved. As noted by the U.S. Department of Justice announcement, "SCOTT TUCKER was sentenced to 200 months in prison for operating a nationwide internet payday lending enterprise that systematically evaded state laws for more than 15 years in order to charge *illegal interest rates as high as 1,000 percent on loans.* TUCKER's co-defendant, TIMOTHY MUIR, an attorney, was also sentenced, to 84 months in prison, for his participation in the scheme. In addition to their willful violation of state usury laws across the country, TUCKER and MUIR lied to millions of customers regarding the true cost of their loans to defraud them out of hundreds, and in some cases, thousands of dollars" [emphasis added].[10]

It *is* a jungle out there—and you have to stay alert, be disciplined, and be aware of the traps.

AUDIT YOURSELF

Just as Ron Lieber did with the Trim app to uncover monthly fees he'd forgotten he was paying, it's always good to perform regular self-checks on your spending habits. There's that governor again.

Here is a short checklist of things to make sure you remember:

- Read the fine print before subscribing to any service.
- When a business asks for a credit card number (even if you're signing up for a free trial), assume that
  - The business plans on billing you.
  - The business is likely to bill you without advance warning.

- Keep an eagle eye on monthly statements to identify charges you may have forgotten about. (Even small ones add up over time.)
- Set calendar reminders for when free trials expire so that you aren't unexpectedly charged for a service you no longer want.
- Pay for subscriptions with a credit card to get stronger consumer protection than you would by paying directly through your bank account.
- Consider setting up a separate checking account or credit-card account to keep all your digital purchases in one place (just remember to pay the balance in full each month).
- If you prefer to farm out tedious tasks, consider using Trim or Truebill or some other service to ferret out unwanted fees and kill "zombie" subscriptions that live on despite efforts to cancel.

Okay, we've started our financial fitness regime with a light workout of eliminating nuisance and hidden costs and spur-of-the-moment shopping. Now let's get ready for some heavier lifting.

Debt Begets More Debt

Think what you do when you run in debt: you give to another power over your liberty.

—BEN FRANKLIN

Thinking before you click to buy that shiny new bauble, even if you can't afford it, probably seems like basic stuff. And you're right, it is basic. But if living within your means is so basic, then why have so many people accepted the dangerous myth that we should freely use consumer debt to buy the things that will supposedly make us and our loved ones happy?

If your expenses exceed your income, the only ways to fund that gap are either drawing on savings or incurring debt. That's just the way it works. Unfortunately, many Americans opt to incur debt. Adding more debt increases your interest costs, which puts more pressure on you to increase your income—and getting a raise, as everyone knows, is never easy. Ignoring the simple math involved here is devastating to millions of Americans today. The buildup of debt by the federal government, private corporations, and we-the-people has reached levels that are astounding and that should be alarming to us all.

The following numbers could haunt your dreams if you let them. They're from the nonpartisan Federal Reserve. In the last quarter of 2018, total household debt went up for the eighteenth consecutive quarter and is $869 billion (6.9 percent) higher than the previous high in total debt during the first months of the Great Recession. *Our cumulative household red ink is more than one-fifth higher than it was in the third quarter of 2013.* New car loans hit $584 billion, the *highest level in the 19-year history* of the Fed keeping these data.[1]

Here are some other numbers to consider:

- The rate of credit-card holders falling into serious delinquency with their accounts spiked in the fourth quarter of 2018, rising sharply for older borrowers.
- Average total debt per household topped $50,000 in the third quarter of 2018 for the first time since 2010 and stayed above that level in the fourth quarter, at $50,210. At least average household debt is still below the precrisis high of $53,000.
- Auto loans hit an all-time high in the fourth quarter of 2018.[2]

Adding insult to injury, beware the debt death spiral. When you rack up credit-card debt and late payments, that wrecks your credit score. Once you have a lower credit score, you will pay more to borrow money for basics such as a home or a car. Stated simply: debt begets more debt. Again, that's just how it works.

We all need to return to the thrift and common financial sense that was the essence of American greatness and long ago woven into our cultural DNA. Don't believe me? Let's turn to Benjamin Franklin for his money advice. He had this figured out long before I and other financial authors showed up.

Benjamin Franklin wrote about four basic principles of thrift:

1. "Gain may be temporary and uncertain, but ever while you live, expense is constant and certain." Hope is not a financial strategy; we must be realistically and conservatively prepared for the expenses of living and realize that such costs are more than we anticipate.
2. "Never keep borrowed money an hour beyond the time you promised." When you take on debt, time costs you money.

3. "Think what you do when you run in debt: you give to another power over your liberty." Ben Franklin understood that debt is a prison. It ruins lives, relationships, and families.

4. "He that is of the opinion money will do everything may well be suspected of doing everything for money." Align your money decisions with the values you wish to live by. How much do you really need? Counter the temptation to click with the mental trick of remembering how happy you will be if you retain self-control of your budget. "Never let the things you own end up owning you," goes the famous line in the film *Fight Club*.

RESPONSIBLE DEBT

There is such a thing as responsible debt, certainly. If you have enough money for a down payment on a home, and if the amount of the loan is not out of proportion to your income stream—and if you have at least a small nest egg to fall back on in case of job loss or personal emergency—then a home mortgage is smart. It is a responsible way to buy and invest over time in shelter for you and your family. In addition, a secured debt, such as a mortgage, is always safer than an unsecured debt, such as a credit-card balance because the lender has collateral. Still, such a serious commitment should scare you silly, unless you've got your ducks in a row. *Never* take out a home loan on faith that your personal finances, or the economy in general, will get better. *Always* avoid *balloon mortgages* like the plague they inevitably are, as you will see when we dig into them in Chapter 4.

Let me add that it is also possible to have "responsible" credit-card debt. But only if you can pay off what you owe each month. Seriously. This is the only 100 percent certain way to avoid the debt trap. A hugely concerning problem for our society is that many people—tens of millions of people—effectively use debt as a way to expand their lifestyles. This inevitably costs individuals more than they bargained for. Our country at large has become a roiling ocean of debt in which consumers flail and sometimes suddenly drown in high debt. This is what happened during the Great Recession that began in the fall of 2008 and kept taking households down for the better part of a decade.

TYPES OF CONSUMER DEBT

Consumer debt trends are documented by the Federal Reserve, the institution charged with maintaining the stability of our financial system. I follow these data closely. I look at the charts—and while the renewed economic growth of the first two years of the Trump administration is encouraging, our debt crisis is still growing. The Fed's chart of revolving debt, for instance, shows a gigantic mountain built up since 1968 when credit cards came into popular use (Figure 3.1).[3]

Credit cards aren't the only type of revolving debt, although they are by far the largest component. Another major type is the home equity line of credit (HELOC), in which a home is held as collateral for a loan. Human nature being what it is, millions of mortgage holders tapped their HELOCs for unnecessary and unaffordable luxuries (such as new top-end kitchens and in-ground pools) during the real estate boom. After the 2007–2009 mortgage loan crisis, when home values plummeted like meteors crashing to Earth, the number of home equity loans given out by banks declined steadily. Total household debt also declined for 19 consecutive quarters starting in late 2008 as consumers felt forced into curtailing their spending. This mass "deleveraging" of debt was unprecedented in the history of records kept by the Fed. But, inexorably, starting in 2013, total household debt began to rise again. As it turned out,

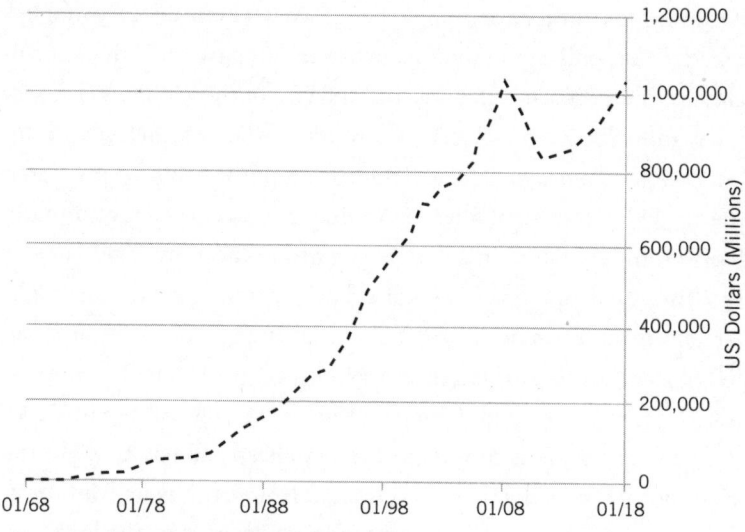

FIGURE 3.1 **Credit-card debt, 1968–2018.**
Fed data only go back to 1968, which is around the time credit cards came into widespread use (late 1950s to early 1960s).

credit cards were now being used in the same way that home equity loans had been before the crisis—to keep spenders afloat. People in large numbers were again opting not to live within their means. In many ways, government policies abetted this irresponsible spending. Artificially low interest rates by the Fed gave banks plenty of cheap cash to lend out to credit-card holders. To be sure, many people in need turn to borrowing to keep the wolf from the door, but as with many of these situations, the wolf will find another way into the house. In the words of Warren Buffett, "If you buy things you do not need, soon you will have to sell things you need."

DRIVE OVER THAT BALLOON IN THE ROAD

After the recession, the Fed lowered interest rates and kept them low for almost a decade to stimulate spending and "reinflate" the economy. It should have been warier of what a cycle of "easy money" and deficit spending brought us in the recent past: the dot.com collapse of the 1990s and the housing collapse of the 2000s. What sector is most likely to collapse as a result of the current cycle? I am not *that* good a prognosticator. But, if you pushed me, I'd say watch the auto loan industry, where subprime loan defaults are ominously blossoming. As noted in a *Business Insider* column by Wolf Richter in 2018, the delinquency rate for subprime auto loans is at its highest rate in more than 20 years and higher than during the Great Recession. "Auto loans to customers with subprime credit ratings—FICO [Fair, Isaac and Company] scores below 620—are risky affairs. During good times and endless cheap money, though, the high interest rates that can be extracted from car buyers who think they have no other options are just too tempting. Now the losses are coming home to roost.

"Big banks have become relatively conservative in this category and are sticklers for things like income verification and other details, which has made room for specialty lenders with fewer such compunctions."[4]

So let's focus on car loans and the big balloon of debt they represent for so many Americans in many walks of life. The total auto debt nationwide, according to the Fed's most recent report, is $1.23 trillion. Yes, trillion dollars. It is ordinarily considered a good thing for the economy when people buy cars, of course. It means jobs for the workers in the auto industry and positive economic effects that ripple out in many ways.

But I must repeat myself: it is bad for the economy and for your household when debt piles up out of proportion to your ability to pay. Car debt has become a prime example of this happening in too many households.

The average new vehicle loan is $30,534, and the average monthly payment is $509, according to Experian's 2018 state of the auto finance market report.[5] The overall delinquency rate (90 days behind in payments) is 4.3 percent. This is lower than the delin-quency rate for student loans and mortgages, but it has been slowly increasing since 2015. A national crisis with delinquent car loans could never be a disaster on the scale of the mortgage loan crisis for the overall economy. Auto lending is simply a smaller business. And Wall Street does not set up as many "packaged" securities and derivatives with car loans that spread around debt like an infection. (Maybe they learned something?) But for the individual car buyer? Delinquency can be a real disaster. One obvious reason is that it is fairly easy for lenders to take back their collateral in case of default. While foreclosing on a home usually requires a long, multistep court procedure, your car is parked right there in your driveway where the "repo man" can snag it.

People with lower FICO credit scores are especially vulnerable when it comes to car loans. After the recession, large banks became more conservative about lending to those with FICO grades equiva-lent to less than a B or C. They strengthened requirements about income verification and assumed schoolmarmish attention to detail in processing such loans. The Fed reported in 2017 a total of about $280 billion of "subprime" auto loans still outstanding in this coun-try. (*Subprime* refers to the borrower, not the lender.) There is no hard-and-fast standard for who is assigned a subprime loan, but gen-erally speaking, it means borrowers with FICO credit scores below 600 to 640 on an 850-point scale. These borrowers must secure a subprime loan if they want to buy a car from a dealer that costs more than they have in their piggy banks. As noted in the Fed's Liberty Street Economics blog,

> Further disaggregating the delinquency rates by the origination credit score of the borrower shows that while the delinquency rates for borrowers with credit scores of 660 or higher appear to be somewhat steady, the subprime delinquency rates are really where the pressure is. This is especially stark when we break out auto finance and bank loans, which shows that the delinquency

rate—even among borrowers in the same credit score bucket—is considerably higher and rising on the auto finance side.[6]

Almost without exception, the interest rate is higher for subprime loans, as high as 20 percent or even higher. The loans are made by lenders that specialize in subprime auto finance. The subprime specialists make their profit by charging a higher interest rate on money they borrow from big banks at the prevailing rate. Recently, three subprime lenders—Summit Financial Corp, Spring Tree Lending, and Pelican Auto Finance—filed for bankruptcy or were forced into it, raising concerns about the whole subprime loan business structure. The allegations made against those companies in court filings make it sound as if the companies themselves were operating one step ahead of the repo man. The words *fraud* and *misrepresentation* were uttered by regulators and prosecutors looking into loans made to people buying "too much car" for their budgets.

There had been evidence of loose standards for making subprime loans for quite some time before these three lenders happened to get tapped by the long arm of the law. For years, regulators and federal agencies have pursued complaints about Santander Consumer, the heavily investigated subprime auto lending arm of the Spanish banking giant. In August 2018, the Consumer Financial Protection Bureau under Trump appointee Mick Mulvaney settled with Santander Consumer USA for predatory lending practices.

Santander agreed to a legal settlement over claims that it allowed borrowers to "make interest-only monthly payments without explaining that doing so would increase the total cost of the loan," according to Reuters, citing three sources familiar with the deal. It also "failed to explain to customers how an insurance policy—known as 'guaranteed auto protection' (GAP)—would not always cover the costs of replacing a car that was destroyed in an accident."[7]

That wasn't all. In 2017, the state attorneys general of Massachusetts and Delaware settled another lawsuit with Santander USA over shoddy subprime loans, with Santander paying $26 million. In Massachusetts, for example, Santander colluded with auto dealers that targeted consumers who couldn't afford the loans. One dealer inflated borrowers' incomes by at least $45,000 a year, according to Maura Healey, attorney general for Massachusetts.

"Yet Santander continued to do business with those dealers and failed to rein in their practices," according to Healey. In some cases, Santander required that some dealers buy back loans that had defaulted, she said."[8] Santander USA has been hit with subpoenas and civil investigative demands from at least 28 state attorneys general over its lending practices.[9]

Car sales keep on rising rapidly in the country, but defaults on car loans keep rising, too. As when an unstoppable force meets an immovable object, something's gotta give. Maybe it will be the subprime loan market. Maybe it should be Americans' fixation on the latest and most luxurious ride they can acquire, unless they can actually afford it.

RAISING RESPONSIBLE SPENDERS

Debit spending has become a way of life in America, and we have begun passing it down as a cultural heritage. A good number of us are even handing credit cards to our kids before they have any income. A 2017 T. Rowe Price survey showed how children are increasingly being given access to credit cards. Only 4 percent of children aged 8 to 15 had access to credit cards in 2012. Five years later, 18 percent of kids in this group had credit cards.[10]

Again, there is a big difference between *responsible* and *irresponsible* spending habits that parents pass along to their children. If done responsibly, giving children/dependents a credit card can help them build credit before they attain financial independence. This will provide them with the future gift of lower interest rates and insurance rates and an easier time of renting an apartment. The parents must have good credit first; otherwise, they cannot provide the child with good credit.

So let's say you've worked hard for a strong credit rating, and you want to add your child as an authorized user on a credit card. Just remember, the child will have the same spending power as you but none of the financial responsibility for the bills. I suggest that parents lay down ground rules and make sure that they are followed. This is what I have done with my current teenagers. If you don't think your young one is ready for this, try the "sock drawer" method of helping him or her build good credit. Add your dependent's name as an authorized user, but do not provide him or her with access (hide the card in the sock drawer). By using the card for small charges every few weeks and paying the balance off in full each month, you can build your child's credit without risk to your own. Another option when deciding for your child might be a secured credit card; this is an account with a low limit of credit, secured by your deposit of cash. You might put $250 on the card and permit your kid to spend as wisely as he or she is able with that. Lessons can be learned, but no major harm will be done.

Debit cards that allow kids to spend money deposited in their bank account on the first of each month are a modern way of providing a cash allowance. Kids learn to budget their purchases against their balance, and again, no big harm results if they run through their balance in the first week of the month. And it is wise to let them experience lean times until the first of the next month!

If you want to home school your kids to become financially literate about credit, here are a few important facts and principles you will want to share:

- Credit-card companies commonly lure customers with 0 percent interest rates for the first year or so. It is very risky to get into debt during this period because the interest rate can balloon to more than 20 percent when it's over.

- No matter what the interest rate is, *never* carry a balance on your credit card.
- Pay on time. If you're late by 60 days, companies can increase the interest rate as a penalty.

In addition, I strongly recommend reminding your kids (and yourself) to understand from the outset that interest rates can rise according to the national economic situation—not just their personal lives. The Fed has the power to lower interest rates to combat the effects of recession and to raise them to prevent inflation. As our economy continues to improve from the Great Recession, rising interest rates are possible. So personal credit-card debt is likely to become even more burdensome in the coming years. Good to know, right?

FINANCIAL HISTORY LESSON

Now that we've addressed the problems of debt and what you must teach your children about it, let's take time for a refresher on recent financial history. It is to each of our benefit to know and understand the basic threads. How did we get here? How did lending get to be so easy and destructive for citizen consumers? Why doesn't our government teach financial responsibility to help us protect ourselves?

Back in 1933, in the aftermath of the Wall Street crash of 1929 and the ensuing Great Depression that caused runs on many banks, a law was put into place separating banks into two types—commercial banks (for consumers) and investment banks (for corporations, institutions, and high-net-worth individuals). The 1933 Glass-Steagall Act held commercial banks to very strict standards concerning risk in their investments—thus curtailing opportunities for maximum gains but protecting them as stable repositories for consumers' funds that are insured by the federal government up to certain levels. Over the next 60 years, enforcement of Glass-Steagall regulations gradually weakened as commercial banks pushed and bumped against its limits on what they could do with their own money. Some of you may recall debates in Congress back in the 1990s over the appropriateness of Glass-Steagall to modern-day banking. In late 1999, during the Clinton administration, Congress moved to gut the law. New legislation was passed to allow commercial banks to engage freely in insurance and investment banking with their own money (but not their customers' funds).

Almost immediately, this resulted in the launch of a wave of bank mergers and new types of financial entities and *vehicles*, that is, packaged loans that could be sold and resold repeatedly and often. In September 2000, two giant banks, J.P. Morgan and Chase Manhattan, came together to make the most of these new opportunities. This was the biggest bank merger ever, a $33 billion deal that created a financial institution regulators instantly saw as being "too big to fail"; that is, if the bank went under, it would result in widespread economic disaster. Other mergers quickly followed. Big banks swallowed small banks, and investment banks and commercial banks intermarried.

Things got ugly with the financial upheavals of 2008. On January 11, 2008, Bank of America announced its acquisition of the troubled subprime lender Countrywide Financial Services, crippled by its underwriting of bad mortgages. In the days after the shock waves of the crash, Bank of America swooped in to buy reeling Merrill Lynch on September 14. These deals would not have been possible before 1999. On September 15, 2008, the investment bank Lehman Brothers collapsed.

Then the world's largest insurance company, AIG, stepped into the barrel. AIG had charged into the derivatives market by using credit-default swaps to insure exotic investments such as collateralized debt obligations (CDOs) that were all the rage in markets fueled by the subprime mortgage boom. These credit-default swaps pushed the otherwise profitable company to the brink of bankruptcy.[11] As the mortgages tied to the swaps defaulted, AIG was forced to raise millions in capital. When stockholders got wind of the situation, they sold their shares, making it even more difficult for AIG to cover the swaps. AIG found itself so destabilized that on September 16 the Fed and Treasury released $85 billion in bailout money for AIG to stay afloat (and later another $100 billion).

Then the hyperaggressive Bank of America found itself in trouble as it tried to juggle the impossibly complex, interwoven, and overleveraged investment products it now owned. By October, the Fed and Treasury classified Bank of America as too big to fail and released $45 billion in bailout loans. At the same time, General Electric fessed up and suddenly told the Fed that it was on the brink of being unable to roll over its short-term debt with lenders. No wonder, the nation's second Wall Street "crash" occurred on September 29, 2008. On that day, the Dow Jones Industrial Average registered the largest point drop in history (up to that time) for a single day of stock trading: 777.68 points.

Lawmakers felt compelled to do *something* to rein in banks and protect consumers amid the financial crisis and recession. The landmark Dodd-Frank Act of 2010 was the Democrats' answer and passed on a largely partisan basis. The law established the Consumer Protection Financial Bureau (CPFB), designed by then Harvard Professor (later U.S. Senator) Elizabeth Warren to ostensibly protect consumers but also with an unaccountable structure that federal courts later found unconstitutional.

As some readers know, in my first book, *Going Public*, I documented my role in many of these controversies, including finding a way to make the *Volcker rule* an effective tool for managing risk by curtailing riskier investments on the parts of the banks that are repositories for our money. Dodd-Frank also established an intra-agency star chamber named the Financial Stability Oversight Council housed at the U.S. Treasury that I called in *Going Public* a "Frankenstein-ish super regulator staging a hostile takeover of the SEC's [Securities and Exchange Commission's] role in regulating American's mutual funds, investment advisors and other investment management firms."

Dodd-Frank brought new and far tougher restrictions on banks, with annual *stress tests* to gauge their stability in the event of another crisis. In this period, home mortgage lending became so heavily regulated and requirements for down payments so intimidating that millennials and others without substantial incomes turned to apartment life. From 2008 to 2011, total credit-card debt also declined. Ultimately, many asset managers stepped in to provide all types of credit in a much more risk-focused manner than the banks ever had. With Dodd-Frank sidelining the banks through higher capital requirements, the lending field was freed up for more business-savvy lenders.

The crisis seemed to encourage more responsible spending by consumers—I know it did for me. You are free to draw your own conclusions. Mine is that free markets, effective enforcement of existing rules, and responsible spending are all best practices.

In 2016, the political pendulum swung hard to the Republicans and President Donald Trump, who had made a campaign pledge to "dismantle" Dodd-Frank. He could not deliver on that one, but in May 2018 he signed a measure that was the product of years of bipartisan negotiation and called it just the "first step." Midsized banks (often known as *community banks*) and credit unions now face much less scrutiny and are exempt from the annual stress tests. Banks with less than $10 billion in assets are once again free to engage in trading with their own money (through a holding company).

Trump appointed Congressman Mick Mulvaney—a consistent critic of the CPFB—to head it. There was a lot of political scrapping over that because Democrats seemed to have hoped that an unelected head of the agency would be in charge forever.

Once he took charge, Mulvaney:

- Immediately stopped hiring at the CFPB, stopped collecting fines from violators, and ordered a review of all active investigations.
- Shut down public access to the CFPB's online database of consumer complaints.
- Fired its entire advisory board in June 2018 and replaced it with a new board in September.
- Issued a series of decisions siding with payday lenders being prosecuted for charging high rates of interest.

In my view, like it or hate it, the CFPB was never needed. It duplicates the same consumer protection rules enforced by other well-established agencies, including the SEC, and has little to add for the taxpayer's investment. Rather than waste time neutering its powers, simply eliminate the agency.

YOUR MOVE

So whatever cycle of regulation and enforcement we are in, your basic situation remains: you need to protect yourself against debt. Once you have debt, you need to deal with it. If you have too much debt to pay off, it may take several years and a lot of sacrifices to reverse that.

Here are the steps I recommend you always follow:

1. **Stick to one credit card.** Pay it off monthly. Use cash whenever you can. Remember, paying only the minimum amount due on a card will mean that you pay a lot more, for a long time. For example, if you pay only the minimum payment due each month on a $1,000 balance with an 18 percent annual percentage rate (APR), you could take an estimated seven years or longer to pay it off while paying an additional $1,000 to $1,730 in interest.

2. **Become a smart car shopper.** New cars depreciate faster than a speeding Ferrari, so research the options: used, pre-owned, and dealers' test-drive vehicles. Look on Craigslist and use CarFax. (You must subscribe, so keep an eye out. See Chapter 2.) Consider one car for your household, if possible. How about riding a bike? (You won't have to pay for parking, either!)

3. **Reduce your housing costs.** Downsize if you can't afford your home. Take on a roommate. Buy a duplex (you'll save on taxes too). That's a topic for Chapter 4.

4. **Pay attention to your credit reports.** You can probably get your credit report for free from your bank. Credit reporting agencies must also by law provide you with a free credit report once a year. Pay attention to those little notices attached to your bank statement that tell you if you are spending more or less than you deposit from your earnings—and then spend less.

5. **Set an amount for discretionary spending each month.** Do this to cover the unavoidable things that come up and the occasional must-have latte. Don't use credit to go over that limit.

If you have excessive credit-card debt, you must form a concrete plan to dig out. Bring your brains and your self-interest to the table; don't just sign up for the first credit-card counseling service you hear about. It's like dating. Watch out for big promises and smooth operators. Stick to the simple math and commonsense that gets lost in the money game: paying back your debt requires spending less, making more, and making sacrifices to do both. Yes, you should pay off your higher-interest-rate cards first, and you can consolidate your debt onto one card where you pay zero interest for a set amount of time. This can simplify the task, but the task remains—restructure your behavior so that you don't go further into debt, and pay off your balances. Then you can build your personal balance sheet.

Some options include:

- Set up an accountability partner, a trusted friend or family member who will hold you to your budget and perhaps in special situations loan you an amount to pay off the debt if you are accountable to your plan.
- If you have, ahem, an excess personal inventory of goodies—say, a third car, a second set of golf clubs, or two Rolex watches—sell them. It is likely you couldn't afford them in the first place.

Most of all, when it comes to credit-card debt, like speeding on a country road with your arm out the window, paying blackjack at the casino when you're drunk, or planning your bachelor party for Las Vegas, don't ask for trouble. Believe me, it will find you.

The Mortgage Trap   4

We shape our buildings, and afterwards our buildings shape us.
—SIR WINSTON CHURCHILL

Home is a concept that draws on some of our deepest emotions. It is closely tied to our ideas of family, security, and the American Dream itself. Because it carries a symbolic importance much greater than most of the big financial decisions we make, the dream of homeownership can lead to major financial mistakes.

In fact, it is a cultural myth that to have a good home, you must own it. It is even more misguided that so many Americans see it as an essential step toward wealth and status. In fact, the number one financial sinkhole for working families is a monthly mortgage payment that is simply too high. "It's time to move beyond the subprime mortgage meltdown and ask a more fundamental question," Clive Crook wrote in a brilliantly prescient essay published in 2007 in *The Atlantic*. "Is it good for society that Americans aspire to own homes, rather than merely live in them?"[1]

Okay, that is a tough question. But I know this: you need to take a hard look at all your options before you anchor your financial ship to mortgage debt. In many ways, mastering money is about becoming the master of your mind and sorting out financial truth from truisms and myths. This is what this chapter is about.

Unfortunately, there is a scam out there that preys on our desires and perpetuates the homeownership myth. It starts with the federal government, which makes it easy for Americans to get mortgages they can't afford. The two government-sponsored mortgage entities, the Federal National Mortgage Association ("Fannie Mae") and the Federal Home Loan Mortgage Corporation ("Freddie Mac") guarantee mortgages so that Americans get 30-year loans that are unavailable in most other countries. When the Fed keeps interest rates artificially low, as it did after the 2008 financial crisis, it saturates the American economy with cheap money that can be lent to home buyers who probably should not take the plunge. All of this is effectively a subsidy for home buying. Developers and the real estate industry love it because they can keep developing and selling. Unregulated mortgage brokers and financing companies love it too because the more loans they write, the more they profit. The result? Housing demand rises, and so do home prices, eventually into crazy land, as during the last boom and devastating crash in 2008. When housing markets "adjust," however, millions of everyday people who played by the rules and scrimped for their down payment can be trapped. Renters can move to lower-cost housing. Homeowners— or, more accurately, those who owe mortgage debt—are frequently anchored in place. Foreclosure is often the result.

I am hopeful that with the introduction of smarter policies, this will change substantially in the years ahead. But the reality is this: standards of living and incomes in America haven't risen enough to justify our high rate of homeownership, which is more or less equivalent to post–World War II levels (a time of unmatched American prosperity). People are going deeply into debt for their homes, and the federal government is mostly to blame.

THE MONEY EARTHQUAKE OF 2008

Numerous books have provided scathing and unforgettable reporting on the abuses of the mortgage "gold rush" preceding the 2008 crash. Investment banks such as Merrill Lynch held trillions of dollars of subprime mortgages on their books in the form of esoteric investment instruments. At the end of a long chain of financial wheeling and dealing were unsuspecting citizens who had bought into the subprime mortgage scam—typically with a great deal of naiveté. Sadly, before the crisis, Congress had mandated that banks make more subprime loans to "underserved" populations, which fueled the rush to provide mortgages to people who were unable to weather a financial storm.[2]

In the book by former Lehman honcho Lawrence McDonald (with Patrick Robinson), *A Colossal Failure of Common Sense: The Inside Story of the Collapse of Lehman Brothers*, McDonald recounts an undercover trip to Los Angeles to check out New Century, one of the "mortgage factories" selling billions of dollars of mortgages every month, many of them subprime. Lehman Brothers and other players on "the Street" (Wall Street) knew at this point in the market that "no one can afford to hold onto the scalding hot potato of subprime mortgages that cannot be sold."

McDonald was sitting at a restaurant next to the New Century offices with his partner, waiting for the "body builders"—the buff, slick mortgage salesmen with gleaming teeth—to swing by for drinks after work. What the men found at New Century was a factory churning out thousands of subprime mortgages to unsuspecting buyers.

"Worse yet, the interest rate resets were about to kick in. We'd seen the documents. Hundreds of thousands of poor people were about to see their monthly payments rocket up from $800 a month to possibly $2,400 a month, maybe more. It had to be a house of cards, because these people could not afford that much," McDonald wrote. The New Century drama as it played out in McDonald's book is a fascinating example of what went down not only at Lehman Brothers but also in the entire financial sector.[3]

Stories of Foreclosure

We all make financial mistakes. I have pulled some doozies, such as renting an expensive one-bedroom Manhattan apartment during my first years working at a law firm, when all I needed was a studio because I was never home. In my pro bono legal work at Kirkland & Ellis, I've talked to low- and moderate-income Americans who are facing tough financial choices. I have seen the worry in their eyes and heard the pain in their voices.

The stories reach across every state and demographic. Take Brian Burns of Las Vegas, who bought into the Nevada housing boom in 2004, moving into a 3,500-square-foot house bought for $250,000 in 2004 and selling it for $650,000 three years later. Flipping houses at that time was easier than selling beer on a hot Sunday afternoon at Yankee Stadium. During the boom of the early and middle 2000s, financial gurus pushed the idea of using leverage (debt) to buy houses that could be spruced up and sold to the next sucker. The advice that sold the most books pushed the idea of buying as much real estate as possible, using as much of other people's money as possible.

Brian was fortunate to have sold his investment property, but he was still overleveraged. As National Public Radio (NPR) reported at the time, "[Brian] decided to keep it in the bank and buy another, smaller house in a brand-new development in the town of Henderson, Nevada. Sure, the stucco tract-style housing didn't have a whole lot of charm, but Burns didn't care. He persuaded some of his friends to buy other houses in the neighborhood. He had cash in the bank, excellent credit, and he put no money down."[4]

Many people who relied on debt in the hopes of building a real estate "empire" overextended their financial reach. But real estate investments are just one part of the tale. Homeowners who depended on the same mogul-based advice for buying their own homes also set their families up for financial disaster.

In 2017, Nobel Prize–winning economist Robert Shiller wrote about how get-rich hype and promises from house-flipping gurus seized consumers' imaginations with envy-inducing narratives about "smart investors who were bold enough to take a position in the market." A new gold rush was on, and the purveyors of these stories made it seem like riches awaited anyone audacious enough to take the chance.

As Shiller notes, real estate flipping "gurus" at the time urged amateur investors to leverage "other people's money" to buy and redevelop properties. In other words, the game was to borrow as much as you can. Consumers heard a constant drumbeat about the upside of leverage in seminars and informercials but not much about the perils of leverage during the big kind of price drops that were just around the corner.[5]

Shiller's analysis shows how our brains are susceptible to over-confident or optimistic biases—we want to believe we have greater control over a project or decision than common sense and evidence dictate. This is a common problem in mastering money and certainly in mortgage holding.

So it was with Brian.

By 2009, Brian's house was worth only $140,000. The crash had devastated his freelance business. Money was tight. Brian stopped paying his mortgage, which destroyed his great credit rating. Brian "let the bank take his house and moved to Oregon to start over," the story reported. By 2016, Brian had returned to Las Vegas, where he rented a small apartment.[6]

Then there's Guillermo Gallindo and his wife of Revere, Massachusetts, who bought a house at the top of the market in 2005 for $450,000 with 5 percent down and a monthly mortgage payment of about $2,000. By renting out the top floor, the Gallindos could afford their mortgage payments—until the economic downturn cut into Guillermo's own working hours and his renters fell on hard times. Meanwhile, the interest rate on his adjustable rate mortgage crept higher.

The crash cut the value of his home in half, and the bank wouldn't renegotiate his mortgage. Guillermo believed in the American Dream and wanted to keep his house—his roots—until he could pass it on to his daughter. But after months of struggling to stay in their dream house, the Gallindos could no longer pay the mortgage, and the bank foreclosed. As of 2016, they rent a two-bedroom apartment.[7]

Naturally, homeowners with subprime loans with higher interest rates were hit even harder than other homeowners during the 2008 crisis and will be disproportionately foreclosed on in future recessions. During the peak of the boom, single women were the fastest-growing demographic taking out mortgages, particularly subprime ones. A 2008 *New York Times* profile of determined, hardworking single mothers Kue McIntyre and Anjanette Booker and their Belair-Edison neighborhood in Baltimore contained many interesting insights. Belair-Edison was a fragile but promising neighborhood comprised largely of single African American women with families buying their first homes. Many of these mothers acquired their first mortgage as a subprime loan from private lenders targeting aspirational home buyers who lacked good credit.[8] In 2006, most of the neighborhood's 6,400 homes were owner occupied.

The people of Belair-Edison worked, raised families, and believed that homeownership would secure their economic safety net. But the reality was different. When the real estate bubble burst, salon owner Booker saw her adjusted monthly mortgage payment "balloon" from $841 to $1,769; Kue McIntyre defaulted on her mortgage after losing her job. She'd taken two subprime mortgages motivated by the best of reasons—to move her family out of a high-crime, gang-troubled area to a safer, better neighborhood. If she had chosen instead to rent in a better neighborhood, Kue would have had better cash flow and more options for riding out a rough spot. Foreclosures were initiated on more than 400 Belair-Edison neighborhood homes in Baltimore between 2007 and 2008.[9]

In the years that it can take for families to begin to recover from a foreclosure, there is incalculable collateral damage—destroyed credit, separation from communities, and career and educational opportunities indefinitely delayed. While it's tempting to assign blame when an American institution such as homeownership goes so awry, who's most at fault is not the point. The point is that foreclosures are an indicator of excessive debt, which devastates individuals and communities. Foreclosures don't just hurt the family that loses their home—they damage the neighborhood, the community, and the economy at large.

The crash also affected more affluent homeowners, who experienced widespread foreclosures as well as financial losses in the form of short sales—selling their houses at a loss. Economists note that it took longer for wealthier mortgage holders to burn through their savings, so this wave of troubles was delayed for a year or two. Unfortunately, middle-class and upper-middle-class African Americans experienced higher rates of foreclosure because they carried more mortgages from private lenders who had targeted minority families during the boom with riskier, high-interest, and adjustable-rate mortgage loans—stimulated by government policies to encourage lending to underserved groups.

Policy analyst Peter Ferrera of the Carleson Center and Heartland Institute has written extensively on the roots of this disaster. In examining where the foreclosure crisis began, Ferrara pinpointed the 1995 housing initiatives of President Clinton: "Under this new Clinton vision, it became federal regulatory policy to force the nation's financial institutions to abandon traditional lending standards for home mortgages, on the grounds that those standards were racially discriminatory, as African Americans and other minorities could not qualify for mortgages to nearly the same degree as whites and Asians."[10]

Prince George's County in Maryland was an epicenter of this middle-class foreclosure crisis. One carefully documented 2012 report by Janell Ross in the *Huffington Post* highlighted the fate of Osita Otigba and his wife, Peace, who lived in Balk Hill, a new subdivision in Mitchelville, a nicely wooded suburb outside of Washington, DC. The Otigbas and their neighbors were African American professionals or business owners. Janell wrote, "This was an impressive lineup in most any community, but here in Prince George's County, the most affluent majority-black county in the United States, the Otigbas and their neighbors were just part of the wave of well-to-do families who arrived in the years before the financial collapse to stake their claim on a 5,000-square-foot version of the American dream."

Sadly, between 2008 and 2012, the Otigbas and five of their six immediate neighbors were underwater on their mortgages, and the Otigbas were living in fear "that an official foreclosure notice will arrive with an order to vacate."

"'I am like a tree that is on the verge of being uprooted by water,' Otigba said, then sighed. 'When that happens, think of all the other parts of the ecosystem that are upset, the streambeds that overflow, the problems that follow. That's what it is like here.'"[11]

Robert Shiller noted that while some may blame homeowners such as the Otigbas for being financially feckless, foreclosure is a social ill with far-reaching consequences. "What would this mean in human terms?," Shiller wrote. "Picture a line of moving trucks extending for hundreds of miles: they are taking the furniture of countless families to storage lockers. Picture schoolchildren saying goodbye to their classmates. They aren't going on vacation: they are being abruptly moved to the other side of town."[12]

Innocence Lost

The big crash that unfolded from 2008–2010 has (incredibly to me) faded from the political discourse. If you aren't paying attention, you'd likely think that its residual effects have vanished as well. But the scars remain for millions of families—families who in many cases drew down their savings, cashed out their retirements, and took on lethal adjustable-rate mortgages without a safety net or plan B. Why? Because they'd been sold on the belief that this was their chance to get in on the dream, to ride the American wealth engine to prosperity. They drank the Kool-Aid, and it was powerful, flavorful Kool-Aid. But several years have passed, and we *should* be wiser.

None of us can afford the luxury of thinking it can't happen here. It can, it did, and it will. My advice is don't get fooled again.

Between 2008 and 2012, more than 6 million families nationwide lost their homes during the foreclosure process or were in the process of doing so, according to the Center for Responsible Lending.[13] Keep in mind that the Fed kept interest rates low (and Fannie Mae and Freddie Mac kept underwriting mortgages) before the crisis, even as the home sector had reached a frenzy.

THE MORTGAGE DECEPTION

The truth is that the last recession and the recklessness that led to it, while devastating and more severe than any in recent memory, was not an anomaly. Whereas foreclosure rates at the time of this book's publication are at prerecession levels, even minor tremors in the economy expose the fragility of home buyers. Every decade or so, the housing market crashes, wiping out family savings, pushing people over the edge, and damaging neighborhoods. In response, interest rates (usually) go up, and lending standards tighten. But then a few years later the Federal Reserve, Fannie Mae and Freddie Mac, the real estate industry, and mortgage brokers all start the cycle again. Case in point, between 2009 and 2011, home foreclosures shattered previous highs.[14] But now the housing machinery is back at it, once again pushing low-interest loans. Fannie Mae and Freddie Mac raised the permitted debt-to-income ratio for home loans in 2017, meaning that prospective home buyers can borrow more and leverage themselves more. This despite being bailed out by Congress after nearly imploding in 2008 because of defaulted loans.[15]

Single-family home sales are the highest in a decade, and home prices are sizzling in most real estate markets nationwide, with prices going up 5, 6, and 7 percent every quarter. The share of income Americans pay in mortgage debt has been steadily inching up since 2014.

In real estate, the sky is not the limit. Sooner or later, prices come down and interest rates go up. Those 3 percent mortgages, if they are adjustable-rate mortgages, will balloon up to 5 or 6 percent, and many people will be forced out of their homes when the monthly payments become too high.

According to the highly respected "How Housing Matters" surveys by the MacArthur Foundation, in 2015 and 2016, more than half of Americans had to make at least one major sacrifice to pay their mortgage or rent.[16] These included getting a second job, deferring savings for retirement, cutting back on healthcare, running up credit-card debt, and even moving to a less safe neighborhood or one with worse schools. One-third of people said they or someone they knew had been evicted, foreclosed upon, or lost their home in the last five years.

I can point to many good reasons for entering, staying in, or returning to the home buying market, for refinancing, or even for buying up. But these are all dangerous decisions unless you truly have your *financial* house in order. Homeownership can be the American Dream or the American Hustle. Through the principles taught in this chapter, I want you to learn how to avoid the latter and save for the former.

Before I explain the financial traps of the mortgage deception, let's find out how this whole cult of the mortgage got started: in the halls of Congress.

THE THIRD RAIL OF TAX REFORM

Commentators and elected officials have variously labeled the home mortgage interest deduction "the most sacred break in the tax code,"[17] "sacrosanct,"[18] the "Third Rail of tax reform,"[19] and "an American birthright."[20] But our Founding Fathers didn't inscribe home ownership into the Declaration of Independence or the Constitution. No marches were held for this "birthright." In many respects, the sacred status of this provision was an accident of history.

In 1913, Congress passed and President Woodrow Wilson signed the Revenue Act, reinstituting the federal income tax. The Revenue Act also allowed homeowners to deduct interest paid on home mortgages. This was a practical, not an aspirational, move: lawmakers wanted to allow taxpayers to deduct interest as a cost associated with generating income if they rented out their houses.

Historians find no evidence that Congress intended to encourage homeownership for its social value before the end of World War II. Homeownership rates then were far lower than today, income taxes were paid by few, and American citizens carried little debt in comparison with our current era.

The home mortgage deduction became a more prominent vehicle for upward mobility after World War II. Homeownership increased as millions of Americans rode the economic expansion upward. Banks and the Fed responded with lower interest rates and easily available 30-year mortgages.

With greater incomes, more Americans were paying federal income taxes. The middle class and upper middle class began to understand how the home mortgage interest deduction allowed them to cut their federal tax bill, lowering their effective mortgage interest rate further. Real estate lobbyists and home builders became outspoken advocates for the deduction. Property taxes were also deductible, a major benefit for homeowners in affluent high-tax states and densely populated communities with higher property taxes.

In 1986, Congress and President Ronald Reagan embarked on a major cleanup of the tax code that resulted in many changes. Policymakers eliminated deductibility for consumer interest paid on auto loans, credit cards, and other major purchases financed through debt. If you don't remember, it may seem too good to be true: there was a time you could deduct interest on your credit-card debt and auto loans from your income on your federal tax return.

Through it all, the home mortgage interest subsidy remained intact. In effect, policymakers told America that the real estate industry was more important than the automobile industry or other forms of economic activity. Then the tax writers added an additional sweetener—*permitting taxpayers to deduct interest on another $100,000 of loans secured by a home equity loan on top of their mortgage.* Contrary to its image, Congress can be awfully generous to U.S. taxpayers and the banks that lend to them to buy real estate.

Little changed on the mortgage interest front until 2018, when President Trump and Congress put together and passed a new tax reform law. The lawmakers took a modestly courageous stand of trimming back the amount of debt eligible for the mortgage interest deduction to $750,000 while grandfathering in the previous $1 million ceiling for homes purchased before December 15, 2017.

In addition to lowering the mortgage deductibility ceiling, the bill limits the deductibility of property taxes and state and local income taxes to a combined $10,000. In states such as New York and California, where home prices and property and income taxes are high to pay for large governments with employees enjoying high salaries and government pensions, this change means that some homeowners faced bigger tax bills beginning in 2018.

DON'T GET CAUGHT IN THE FINANCIAL TRAP OF A HOME YOU CAN'T AFFORD

As we've seen, the U.S. government, the real estate industry, mortgage brokers, banks, and probably your mom and dad and your Uncle Frank have all bought into the mortgage deception. This is not to say that homeownership has no value. I own my home and have lived in it for many years. But the time to consider buying a home is when:

- You have saved enough money for a down payment and still have an emergency fund that will cover six months of expenses.
- You are confident that you can indeed put down roots for at least five years in one spot.
- You're not buying at the top of the market or stretching to take on a mortgage payment larger than one-quarter of your monthly income. You can follow market cycles by tracking local real estate costs and comparing previous market "highs" with current prices.

Whether you currently own, plan to own, plan to sell, or are in financial trouble and aren't sure what to do, I want you to be well equipped to see through the homeownership narrative so that you can better protect yourself. Arm yourself with research and a calculator to navigate these financial traps about homeownership and money.

I label them *traps* because aspects of them can be true and make sense at certain times for some people, *but* if you step in one at the wrong time, it can put a terrible bite into your finances and happiness.

Trap 1: Your Home Will Go Up in Value, Providing a Return on Your Investment

Over a long period of time, it is likely that the value of the home you buy will increase. But if you need or want to move, you may be stuck in your home during a recession or when your local real estate prices are falling. Not only that, but most of the money that you put into your home you never see again. You can't deduct as many of the costs of improvements as you might think. If you're not renting out a room or otherwise producing income with your house, it is hard to offset home-related expenses such as maintenance, insurance, and taxes. Good investments generate income, not expenses.

The money you invest in a house could be otherwise invested in instruments that offer guaranteed or relatively lower risk returns. Various studies show that stocks and bonds have outperformed home values over time. Consumer tax guru Kelly Phillips Erb makes the point in a wonderful column: "While it's true that some homes do appreciate, so do many other assets. If you bought a house for, say, $200,000 thirty years ago, it would be worth $468,375.09 today. While that gain feels impressive, that appreciation is based solely on inflation—which means that, in theory, the same appreciation would have happened with any asset."[21]

Trap 2: You Must Live *Somewhere*, So Don't Buy a Home for the Home Mortgage Interest Tax Deduction

As I've noted in these pages, the benefits of the mortgage interest deduction are highly deceiving. First-time and other homeowners are often thinking, "Okay, I am paying a bigger share of my income for my mortgage than I am comfortable with, but I get these deductions from the taxes I pay to offset it." Consumers are smart shoppers in looking at the cost of a new suit, a car, or medical insurance, which most of us judge on the affordability of the object's price. But in shopping for mortgages, some of us allow our number we would spend on a home to go up because of what is often fuzzy savings on our tax bill. This is a vulnerability that many brokers and Realtors exploit to make the sale.

Many homeowners ultimately find that even with the availability of a mortgage interest tax deduction, their tax return isn't affected because they are better off taking the standard deduction. In fact, only about one-third of taxpayers even have the option of taking the mortgage interest deduction. Even if you qualify for the maximum home buyer tax credit of $8,000, you need to compare that tax benefit with what you could potentially save by renting—and remember that juicy home buyer tax credit can be another arrow in the real estate agent's quiver of pitches. And that's okay, but consumer beware!

Owning a mortgaged house also inflates your debt-to-income ratios. If you had to borrow to buy your home, which most people do, the presence of that debt can weigh on your credit and ability to take out loans for other things, such as a new car. If you have a lot of student debt, that is already affecting what lenders see as your ability to pay. A mortgage will only drive that ratio up. A monthly rental payment could be as much or more than a monthly mortgage payment—but in terms of your credit rating, rent is calculated as an expense, not a debt like a mortgage.[22] The debt you carry makes up a big piece of your credit-rating score.

Trap 3: Renting Is Just "Throwing Away Money"

Reuters finance columnist Felix Salmon emerged during the real estate crisis as a rapier-sharp voice reporting on the mortgage deception. He said of the bias against renting, "There's this weird fallacy that somehow, paying rent is throwing money away, whereas paying a mortgage isn't. But one of the commenters on my blog put it very well when they said that if you buy a house, you're still renting; you're just renting the money to buy the house rather than renting the house itself."[23]

The humble calculator can be a great friend in evaluating renting versus owning. Write down the numbers in two columns: (1) the costs of taking on a mortgage payment, home maintenance, insurance, improvements (if any), and property taxes for three years and (2) the costs of renting for three years, and if there are expenditures you would make for the apartment and not for the house (furniture, electronics), add those to the column. Calculate your tax benefit from taking on the mortgage. Do the math, and compare. If you save by renting, do you have the discipline to salt that money away for the future, or will you spend it? If you will save this money or invest it wisely as I demonstrate later in this book, then you are hardly throwing your money away.

Finally, and perhaps most important, renters are far more mobile. If the local economy tanks, a new job beckons, or you fall in love and want to move to Seattle, your cash is more liquid. The high transaction costs of buying a home have been shown to reduce labor force mobility and even increase unemployment.[24] If you are in a disadvantaged area with few jobs or bad schools, those high costs can keep you there.

Trap 4: If You Encounter Financial Woes, You Can Sell Your House

This trap won't bite if you time everything right and sell your house at a profit that you can use to bolster your financial situation. You then need to be able to move into a rental that will cost you less than your house so that you can use your sales profit to pay down debt and buttress your emergency fund. But having success with this strategy is rare. If you need the money when your house is underwater, obviously selling it won't help at all. And even if you sell at a modest gain, you will be walking away from what the house could make on the market in the longer term.

In many cases, as I've shown in these pages, you got in a hole because you took out a mortgage you couldn't afford and used your emergency fund for a down payment. I've also shown how volatile the real estate market is. The same economic storm that washes out your property values can be the one that takes out your job as well.

When you sell, your capital gains above $500,000 from selling the house are taxed (if you are filing jointly and have used the house as your main domicile for two of the last five years).[25] But if you sell your house during a tough time, even if you do not (and probably should not) buy another property, you will still pay taxes on the gains you made in selling your house. The bottom line: don't look at your house as a financial safety net. Don't buy a house until you have your savings safety net and other low-risk investments in place.

Trap 5: Federal Programs Make It Safe to Buy a House with a Very Low Down Payment

The Federal Housing Administration (FHA), Veterans' Administration (VA), and U.S. Department of Agriculture (USDA) offer instruments that make it easier for people with moderate incomes or job-loss issues to get a mortgage with small or even no down payments on the home. The FHA, for example, insures mortgages backed by down payments as low as 3.5 percent, so you might think that buying a house with a low down payment is relatively safe. You will have more of your own cash liquid for your use. Yes, you can leverage the small down payment for big gains in home value down the road, but until years pass, you will be carrying roughly $96.50 of mortgage debt for every $3.50 of home equity. When you borrow most of the cost of the house, you have almost no equity.

According to Joseph Gyuorko, chairman of the real estate department and the director of the Zell/Lurie Real Estate Center at the University of Pennsylvania's Wharton School:

> The less equity you have in your home, the greater the chance that a fall in prices will leave you owing more than the house is worth. Negative equity sometimes leads to mortgage defaults, and when buyers default, they lose not just their down payments

but also closing costs and the value of any improvements they've made to their homes. Even if buyers don't default, they may not be able to afford to move, because they have to pay off their old home loans to get new ones.[26]

Even with a small down payment, there are many other costs that you must be aware of when pursuing homeownership, such as closing costs, real estate taxes, fees, and moving costs, that add 2 to 5 percent to the home's total purchase price.

Additionally, these federal programs may not last forever in their current form. These initiatives make it easier for more people to go into debt, which is a huge threat to our well-being individually and as a nation. Should another economic crisis occur, all this debt could crash the FHA and potentially the VA insurance programs. In 2012, the FHA nearly went bankrupt. It has increased its reserves since then, but every financial crisis in our history teaches us not to regard federal involvement in the mortgage market as worry free. Why not simply save more over time and buy a house when you can truly afford it? That's the kind of commonsense that is all too rare in the personal finance debate.

Trap 6: You Can Pass Your Home on to Your Children

I admire the generosity and integrity of parents who have this in mind when they get a mortgage. But this simply isn't a reason to buy a home. Why? It is a fool's errand to predict the future behavior of people, even those you love. "While physics and mathematics may tell us how the universe began, they are not much use in predicting human behavior because there are far too many equations to solve," remarked the late genius physicist and author Stephen Hawking in an interview for his book *The Grand Design*.

Here are some nasty ways your best-laid plans could have unexpected consequences:

- If your adult child is married, he or she could lose the house in a divorce. You could end up being unwelcome in the house you once owned.
- Your adult child could owe gift taxes.
- Your adult child could lose his or her job or sustain a loss in income and encounter the same money challenges I've written about in this chapter.

The Great Recession revealed an uncomfortable but important truth: we can't necessarily trust the institutions—the Fed, the mortgage lenders, and the financial moguls—that we had depended on to guide us. Mastering money means learning to think more independently, to reject harmful narratives, and to act in your own financial best interest. A home can be all the things you want it to be: sanctuary, safety net, and an investment for the future. Like anything really worth having, though, you'll only achieve this through smart, sound planning.

The Lottery Disaster and Other Hidden Taxes

A more useful bit of counsel would have been that buying a lottery ticket is fun but financially foolish. A punter buying a Powerball ticket has a 1 in 292m chance of winning the jackpot. Buyers are around four times more likely to be killed by an asteroid impact this year. Lotteries are designed to be a bad deal, hoovering up participants' money in order to plug state budgets and fund good causes.

—*THE ECONOMIST*[1]

THE COST OF HIDDEN TAXES

As you work on limiting the outflow to help build your personal balance sheet, remember that hidden taxes—both those we indirectly choose to pay and those that are attached to everyday purchases—can sap your efforts. The worst hidden tax is the lottery, because it is a government-sponsored program to reduce your wealth. Next up are government-imposed taxes such as sales taxes that hit lower-income Americans harder than wealthier citizens. Each state has its own laws for the amount of sales tax charged and which transactions fall under the sales tax (a few states do not have a sales tax). Excise taxes are additional taxes on a specific activity such as buying cigarettes or alcohol or engaging in sports betting. The cost per person in each state for sales and excise taxes combined ranges from about $600 to well over $2,000. The Tax Foundation offers informative and useful charts on these costs at https://files.taxfoundation .org/20190206091531/SalesTaxesPerCapita-Final-01.png.

Is it any wonder that government encourages us to spend for a "consumer" society? Each time you buy something, you pay sales tax in addition to the cost of the item. Avoiding these hidden taxes can speed you on your way to personal wealth.

THE LOTTERY

State lottery programs are a form of invisible taxation on middle- and low-income households that is a national disgrace. State lotteries take your money without *making sure* that you know the odds of winning or how your money is being used. Citizens spend $80 billion per year on lottery tickets, and the odds against winning anything other than a few bucks are astronomical. "Last year Americans spent a total of $73.5 billion on traditional lottery tickets, according to the North American Association of State and Provincial Lotteries. Add in electronic lottery games and that figure is $80 billion," reported CNN Business in 2016. "[L]ow income players spend a much larger percentage of their income on tickets than wealthy players."[2]

As with other trends in our economy discussed in these pages, the government isn't interested in your welfare or in being honest about what is going on with state lotteries. Consumer beware—big time.

Since the beginning of the modern lottery, lawmakers have justified their lotteries by telling us that they dedicate the revenues to social and educational programs. There is twisted logic here when you look more closely. The states are selling the PR appeal, not the reality of lottery dollars doing good. Studies have exposed the role of lotteries in gambling addiction, revealing that lotteries are disproportionately purchased by poor and low-income residents, that states vary widely in the accountability of how they spend lottery revenues, and that state advertising does a terrible job of making transparent the bad odds of winning.

In this chapter, I'll explain why lotteries are undermining our already poor savings rates and leaving us exposed, without safety nets, when the next economic crisis hits. As individuals, we can't exert much control over the global economy, Wall Street, or Washington—but we can control how we use our own dollars. We can have a stronger financial safety net and retirement plan. We can empower ourselves to understand how money works and how to make it work for us, not against us.

A CHECKERED PAST

Lotteries date back to America's origins. In the early years of the republic, the new American government ran lottery games to finance public building projects such as roads, wharves, and even churches. In 1768, George Washington sponsored a lottery to build a road across the Blue Ridge Mountains, but it was unsuccessful. In the year of his death, 1826, Thomas Jefferson obtained permission from the Virginia legislature to hold a private lottery to alleviate his crushing debts. Held by his heirs after his death, it was unsuccessful.[3]

But the lotteries of our time are high-powered marketing and money-raising machines compared to the modest games of the eighteenth century. As policy analyst Kathleen Joyce wrote, "These early lotteries bear little resemblance to the modern state operated lottery. The first lotteries were individually operated and licensed by the individual states. Tickets were expensive by current standards. Lotteries were run for specific purposes, such as the construction of a hospital or road, and they ceased operations once the required funds had been raised."[4]

Authorities uncovered massive scandals in the popular lottery run by Louisiana in the 1870s, including bribery and rigged outcomes. Opinion turned against lotteries, and states closed down assorted gambling and lottery operations. The federal government outlawed use of the mail for lotteries in 1890, and in 1895, the government invoked the Commerce Clause to forbid shipments of lottery tickets or advertisements across state lines, effectively ending all lotteries in the United States.

No government body touched a lottery game until Puerto Rico in 1934 and New Hampshire in 1964 (which, lacking a state income tax, stood in need of revenue). Inspired by New Hampshire's positive experience, New York followed in 1966. New Jersey introduced its lottery in 1970, and 10 other states followed by 1975. As of 2018, forty-four states, Puerto Rico, the U.S. Virgin Islands, and the District of Columbia had operating lotteries.

State lotteries in our era are one of the more popular forms of gambling—not only in the United States but also in most developed countries. Lotteries and casinos remain prime examples of how governments have legitimized certain forms of gambling. The even bigger problem: billions are spent by states and casinos on promoting gambling and "growing the market" through advanced analytics and marketing while public education about the odds and risks are minimal.

"Indeed, government approval of gambling necessarily bestows a mark of legitimacy on games of chance," noted one historian.[5] Government sponsorship of lotteries and other forms of gambling "go mainstream" with behaviors such as bookmaking that society had discouraged for decades and longer. New Jersey legalized online sports betting in 2018, immediately luring new gamblers who all told spent over $400 million in the first year. Never forget that the "house" always wins, and in this case, the house is the government tax collector.

Make no mistake, Americans seem to love the lottery. By 1987, the number of states with lotteries had risen to 28, and net revenues—that is, profit above expenses and prize payouts—reached $5.5 billion. By 1997, thirty-seven states and the District of Columbia operated lotteries, and revenues approached $14.2 billion. By 2009, revenues reached $20.2 billion, and by 2015, revenues had soared to $24.6 billion (Figure 5.1). The dollars in total lottery sales are humungous. In 2017, citizens of many states were spending, on average (including non-lottery spenders!), hundreds of dollars per year on lottery. That adds up. (Figure 5.2).

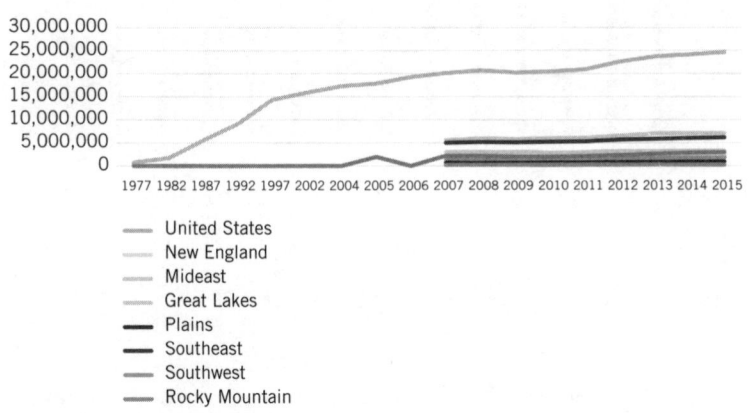

FIGURE 5.1 State and local lottery revenue, selected years 1977–2015 [thousands of dollars][6]

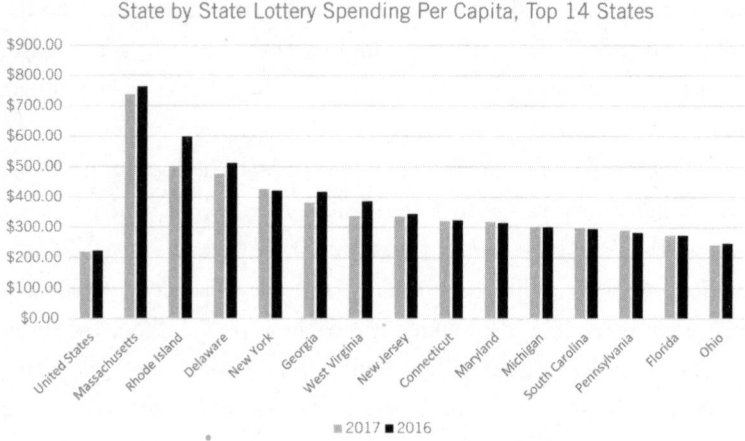

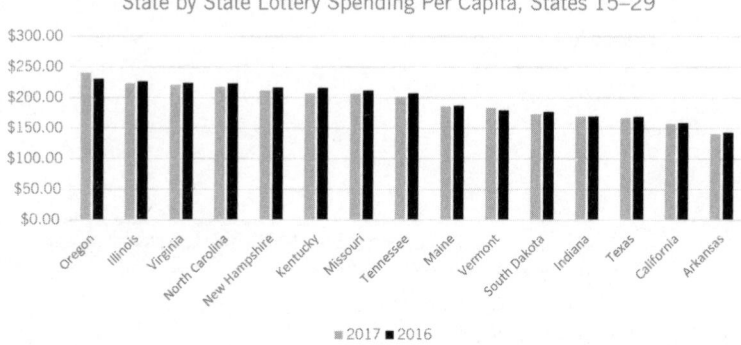

FIGURE 5.2 **State by state lottery spending per capita**[7]

The advice given to Woodward and Bernstein during their investigation of Watergate never goes out of date: follow the money! When you follow the money in lotteries, the truth is plain. "As they are presently constituted, state lotteries are guided by one objective: to raise as much money as possible for state treasuries. This objective is sometimes stated explicitly in state law and often in the annual reports of state lotteries and in state government studies."[8]

HYPOCRISY GAME

If people like the lottery so much and don't mind shelling out a few hard-earned dollars for that tiny shot at a fortune, you may be wondering, "What's the harm?" But the negative effects of the lottery on individual finances are greater than most people realize.

Gambling takes many forms—from dog racing or playing the slots at the casino to betting on the National Football League or the lottery. Taken in its entirety, the trillions of dollars exchanging hands over recreational gambling is alarming and raises many disturbing questions. In this book I am taking aim at the state lottery money machine and its designs to grab your wallet. Why?

- Lottery spending is sponsored by our governments under a charade of doing good. Lottery money is used as tax revenue, lottery tickets are sold everywhere, and no skill is involved. Lottery advertising is not regulated. The game stakes are random with terrible odds.
- Many people who believe that they can't afford to save for college or healthcare are spending thousands of dollars a year on gambling, and lotteries spur people to spend even more. It is well documented that a small percentage of Americans account for most lottery spending: Just 5 percent of consumers account for half of lottery revenues.[9]
- Taxpayers should know the truth about the economics of the lottery and its effect on society because you and I—all of us—*are paying for it.*

THE FIRST HYPOCRISY OF THE LOTTERY IS MOTIVE

Since the beginning of the modern lottery, lawmakers have dedicated lottery net revenues to social and educational programs. By "doing good," lotteries have maintained sufficient public support while becoming one of the leading sources of revenue for governments.

According to the final report issued by the bipartisan National Gambling Impact Study Commission formed by President Bill Clinton in 1997, in virtually every state, "The introduction of lotteries has followed remarkably uniform patterns: the arguments for and against adoption, the structure of the resulting state lottery, and the evolution of the lottery's operations all demonstrate considerable uniformity. . . . The principal argument used in every state to promote the adoption of a lottery has focused on its value as a source of 'painless' revenue: players voluntarily spending their money (as opposed to the general public being taxed) for the benefit of the public good."[10]

But what about this: should our governments promote excessive gambling? Is that a "public good"? Dr. Julia Fleming, chairperson of the Theology Department at Creighton University, brings home the issue of right and wrong in her paper, "Gambling with the Common Good":[11]

> However, in America today, state lotteries are not only regulated by state governments, they are promoted by state governments. This distinguishes lotteries from other forms of activities that communities try to regulate and limit by imposing levies (otherwise known as "sin taxes") on their purchasers. While it is true that governments use both lotteries and sin taxes to raise money, states do not create products such as Wyoming Wine Coolers or Massachusetts Menthols; nor do they issue public service announcements designed to encourage drinking and smoking.

> By contrast, lotteries require the ongoing development of games and promotional strategies, in addition to the administrative costs associated with any governmental activity. For this reason, ethical questions about lotteries in the United States today are necessarily questions about government and its role in promoting the common good. Is running a lottery an appropriate activity for government?

THE SECOND HYPOCRISY
LIES IN THE ADVERTISING

Lottery experts know that revenues expand dramatically after a state lottery is introduced and then level off or even decline.[12] Consumers start spending more when the state introduces new lottery games or the multistate lotto "Megamillions" game. If the lottery is about voluntary spending for a good cause that happens to be fun, then why do states spend millions on gimmicks, new games, huge cash prizes, and misleading advertising and promotion to keep pulling people back?

Lottery ads obfuscate or neglect to mention the odds of winning money, lack disclaimers or warnings, and make many misleading claims. Why? Because lotteries are not bound by the Federal Trade Commission's truth-in-advertising laws. Instead, states are self-regulating, allowing lotteries to get away with misleading and predatory advertising far beyond what private businesses are allowed.[13] Lottery campaigns are outsourced to top marketing and communications firms with state-of-the-art tools for manipulating consumer behavior. In a particularly egregious policy, some states target low-income and minority communities or time outreach for the receipt of Social Security checks.

With all the hype, many studies have shown that states are not accountable for lottery spending, despite their claims.[14] States earmark lottery revenues for education or senior programs, but these dollars often replace existing budget dollars that are redirected elsewhere—in effect, allowing politicians to spend more without raising taxes through the legislature. New York State isolates lottery money in targeted programs that benefit every educational district in the state. But the lottery revenue at best amounts to about 5 percent of a district's budget. In California, lottery revenue covers less than 2 percent of the state's education budget. Many other states, such as New Jersey, "set aside" the revenues for education or the like, but only as an infusion of cash into various agencies.

THE THIRD HYPOCRISY LIES IN TAXES

The lottery is a tax in disguise, and it can really add up for people who can't afford it. Active lottery players tend to finance their purchases by cutting back on necessities, according to economist Melissa Kearney of the University of Maryland. After a state introduces the lottery, people spend more on gambling, and they don't shift money away from other forms of gambling to do so. *They spend more overall.* The bottom third of households shifts about 3 percent of their food expenditures and 7 percent of their mortgage payments, rent, and other bills.[15]

"Effectively, the lottery works like a regressive tax," American Enterprise Institute President Arthur C. Brooks wrote in the *Wall Street Journal* on August 27, 2017. "It might strike you as bizarre that the government spends billions on nutrition and housing programs for the poor while simultaneously encouraging poor people to move their own money away from these necessities and toward the state's gambling monopoly. In fact, that $70 billion in annual lottery revenues is strikingly close to what the government spends on food stamps."[16]

In 2016, legislators in Maine began investigating how the lottery sells "hope to the hopeless," the title of a series of reports by the Maine Center for the Public Interest, which found that lottery sales in Maine's poorest towns were as much as 200 times higher per capita than sales in wealthier areas. The Center also found that lottery sales increased by 10 percent for each 1 percent hike in the state's unemployment rate. It also showed that people receiving public benefits, such as food stamps, aid for needy families, or Medicaid, had spent hundreds of millions of dollars on lottery tickets between 2010 and 2015, enough to take home at least $22.4 million in prizes over $1,000. In October 2016, the administration of Paul LePage, governor of Maine, implemented a rule that removed people who win $5,000 or more through the lottery from the food stamps program.[17]

After all the controversy, Maine's legislature later issued its own report, which did not find specific evidence that lottery advertising and promotion targeted one economic group more than another.[18]

In New York State, taxpayers in the lowest quintile of earners pay more for the lottery on average (about $1,000 per year) than any other form of taxation, according to an analysis by data experts Jeff Desjardin and Max Galka.[19] Another often-quoted study found that poor folks—households earning less than $13,000 per year—spend about a tenth of all their income on lottery tickets.[20]

And if against the odds, you win big, the government doesn't talk about the gigantic tax bite it takes. According to tax journalist extraordinaire David Cay Johnston, "Lotteries are the most heavily financed consumer product in America because after the 38% discount (which depends on interest rates and thus the current time value of money) you then owe taxes at ordinary rates so of the $199 million and assuming no charitable gifts you could net about $110 million, roughly a third of the advertised prize value."[21]

Johnston also points out that lottery revenue is a tax without an opposing lobby: "Because gambling is voluntary, there is little organized opposition to levies on gambling winnings. Contrast that with the ferocious, well-organized and well-financed opposition to income taxes, especially corporate income taxes."

WHAT YOU CAN DO

Is this a Norm Champ grump alert? To be sure, if you can pay your bills, and if you are wedded to the principle of *not losing more than what you can afford* (which in most cases should be modest), then enjoying a game of chance with your friends, such as playing poker or spending a few hours at a casino, is not the end of the world. The lottery odds are even worse than those of the casino.

Lotteries not only act as a tax and exploit low-income citizens, but they're also siphoning millions of dollars we could be saving or investing wisely. They're undermining the already notoriously poor savings rates of Americans, leaving us exposed to tighter budgets, bankruptcies, foreclosures, and poverty when the next economic crisis hits. What starker individual lesson could we have from the Great Recession? It's easy to fall for the lure of the lottery—an average Joe drops a few bucks at a convenience store and becomes rich beyond his wildest dreams. Some who struggle to save may falsely believe that a windfall of cash is the only way to achieve financial security. But the objective of the lottery is not actually to enrich individuals. The reality is that state governments are the real winners, and they cash in by misleading Americans and targeting those who are most vulnerable and least able to afford it. Saving and investing money wisely may not seem as glamorous a path to your financial goals, but it's the only strategy where you're guaranteed to emerge a winner.

Cutting back on addictive behaviors such as gambling and the lottery is rarely easy. We humans essentially "program" our minds to seek to repeat the jolt of endorphins (the brain's "feel good" chemical) we enjoy from the behavior (and in various forms, we all have our endorphin rushes we crave; the trick is managing them). Try these small steps to reduce your legalized gambling:

- Research whether you can access the growing number of savings account–based lotteries that offer much smaller awards for playing but also boost your savings.
- Be aware of people, places, and things that trigger your lottery cravings—for example, the local convenience store or sports betting sites—and replace them with enjoyable alternatives.
- Pick an "accountability buddy" who will check on you as you progress toward a goal (say, cutting spending to $5 per week on tickets as opposed to $20).

- Take up a board game or sport to satisfy your craving to compete and win.

ADDITIONAL HIDDEN TAXES

The government and other entities like to promote our consumer economy because the more you spend, the richer they get. One part of the strategy—hiding the amount of additional money you pay through fees and taxes in disclosure language. To some extent, "you can't beat City Hall"—for the foreseeable future, these kinds of stealth nuisance costs aren't going away. But why not save where you can? Check out these ideas:

- **Sales taxes.** All but five states impose taxes on you at the final point of sale. When you cut spending, you cut the sales tax you pay. If the sales tax on a $200 smartphone is $16, that's 16 more dollars you will have if you put off the purchase. It's like getting cash put in your wallet while you weren't paying attention.
- **Excise taxes.** These are added to products such as tobacco and alcohol that lawmakers see as adding additional health-care and enforcement costs to general society.
- **Property taxes.** When you are taking on a mortgage, no one wants to mention that you will also have to pay property taxes. I know of one website, tax-rates.org (www.tax-rates.org/colorado/alamosa_county_property_tax) that offers an abundance of accurate information about property taxes in every county in the United States. Many adults raising children will typically move to a new community where property taxes are lower after the kids graduate. But you don't have to wait that long to factor taxes into the real cost of buying a home.
- **Phone and cable hidden fees and taxes.** The companies that sell you internet, cable, satellite TV, and mobile phone

services all charge an array of barely disclosed fees and federal and state taxes that substantially increase your bill. And the government likes to keep quiet about the nature of these taxes, which fund all manner of policies, such as extending the internet to rural communities. Cable companies try to sell you a bundle of stations that inevitably includes those you don't watch. Millions of consumers are already cutting their cable or satellite services, switching to streaming devices such as a Roku and an HD antenna for local television stations. Millions more are doing away with their landline phone service and going mobile only (which still can hook into your wallet with barely disclosed fees, minimizing the savings you could enjoy). You have to decide what is best for you and your family. Additionally, if you shop around, mobile and television providers compete aggressively for your business with deep discounts. Often your current cable or satellite provider will cut your basic rate if you threaten to leave.

INCREASE INFLOW

Now that you have learned how to stem your spending outflow, how about giving yourself a raise? The key: avoid gimmicks, and stick with the fundamentals. You've seen those infomercials filling late night with peppy pitchmen selling various wealth-building schemes, such as flipping real estate, stock picking, titles and deeds, what have you. Need I say, buyer beware! I support longer-term goals, which we'll discuss in this part, such as acquiring a new degree or certification, but you can also start increasing your income right away. Volunteer for extra projects at work. Add a shift per week. If you have free time, take on a weekend gig such as dog walking or house-sitting. Hold a garage sale. Sell a set of collectibles. I want you to start training your money muscles in all three subject areas of this book: reducing debt, increasing inflow, and investing.

The Best Social Program Is a Job

There is no worse material poverty, I am keen to stress, than the poverty which prevents people from earning their bread and deprives them of the dignity of work.

—POPE FRANCIS

My father's side of the family has long roots in St. Louis dating back to at least the 1880s, when one of my ancestors moved to St. Louis from Ohio and began a business making heavy leaf springs for wagons and buggies. When the United States moved from horse-drawn conveyances to motor vehicles, springs survived and are now used on heavy over-the-road trucks. This led to the family saying that we were happy our ancestor chose to make buggy springs and not buggy whips! The Champ Spring Company lasted from 1882 until the spring manufacturing business moved offshore, and I had to shut the business down in 2007.

My first job as a teenager was washing dishes at a steakhouse near my father's house where I could ride my bike because I couldn't drive. Later in high school and college, I worked several summers at Champ Spring Company on the loading dock for the shipping manager, Bob Price. It was my first exposure to the world of work outside our family's dysfunctional but comfortable bubble.

Springs for modern trucks weigh anywhere from about 75 pounds to more than 500 pounds. We carried those monsters around to paint them and load them on trucks in 90- to 100-degree summer weather. I took salt tablets to replace the salt lost from sweat. I also drove a forklift truck to load pallets of springs on shipping trucks. I worked alongside people of different socioeconomic backgrounds than my own. It made a deep impression on me. Since then, I've never forgotten what having a stable job means. Work gives people dignity. Work gives people hope.

Both the government and individuals need to take responsibility for getting people to work. In this chapter, I review the considerable and often underappreciated benefits of finding a job, sticking with a job, and acquiring new skills to move up to a better job. I will show how almost any employment is the beginning of the road to upward mobility as you increase your social assets and networks. Work is the bedrock of our economy. And it is the bedrock of your financial security. I am calling on readers to ask themselves, am I doing all I can to increase my skills and get the best job I can?

MAKE WORK PAY MORE THAN WELFARE—ALWAYS

There are real consequences and normal reactions to being unemployed. I would point out, by contrast, that loss of hope and belief in work is unwarranted. Soon after President Trump was elected in 2016, he jawboned corporate executives into keeping more than 700 jobs at the Carrier furnace plant in Indiana instead of shutting it down and moving to Mexico. By the summer of 2018, the *New York Times* was reporting on the high rate of absenteeism and "low morale" among those who *kept* their Carrier jobs. Employees complained that they still didn't trust that their jobs wouldn't disappear—so many of them had just stopped trying to perform. Enough workers called in sick or claimed days off under the Family and Medical Leave Act on some days that the furnace line had to shut down. The *Times* quoted a supervisor, Robin Maynard, who said that he had to suit up and take a spot on the line several times a week to keep the operation going. "The attitude, the demeanor—they're not grateful that they have a job," said Maynard of his fellow workers. "The absenteeism is real bad. A lot of us need our jobs. Others look at it and they don't really care anymore."[1]

We need more people to care about working—and to care about the work they do. We need people to understand the power of work in our lives and never to give up on feeling that power. Yes, the number of unemployed people is low right now, but the statistics do not include those who have given up trying to better themselves at work or those who have given up even looking for work. Actively seeking employment needs to be an ingrained part of our national personality profile for all of us to succeed. The job market will fluctuate. Workers will need to be flexible. If people keep their eyes on the prize and stay alert to opportunities, economic history tells us that they will attain a job one way or another.

After years of decline in manufacturing jobs, the sector began to grow again in the first two years of the Trump administration. In 2017, the economy added 207,000 factory jobs; that number spiked in 2018 as the economy produced another 284,000 factory jobs, according to the Bureau of Labor Statistics. That surge is the highest increase in new workers since 1988.[2] These are good jobs with handsome pay and benefits, jobs that will support families in a middle-class life.

While the Obama administration credited itself with creating more than 11 million jobs, many of those were low-wage service jobs that did not replace the higher-paying jobs lost during the Great Recession. Now these good manufacturing jobs are coming back, and other good jobs will inevitably follow, especially for those who pursue training in emerging fields. Economic history tells us that work is habit forming, but it is a path you must *choose*.

This is why I'm somewhat encouraged that as of 2018, more people are entering the workforce after sitting out, many for understandable reasons, such as being laid off. (When jobless adults of working age stop applying for unemployment insurance, which requires them to job hunt, they are not counted in the workforce.) When the economy was booming in 2000, more than 67 percent of Americans were working or actively looking for work. The rate dipped to as low as 62.3 percent in 2015, rose to 62.9 percent by July 2018, and continued upward to reach 63.2 percent in 2019.[3] This is a small but hopeful sign.

The use of safety-net benefits such as unemployment insurance and the Supplemental Nutrition Assistance Program (SNAP; food stamps) reached historic highs in the Great Recession of 2008–2010, and indeed, that's understandable. The longer trend, however, reveals a considerable expansion in the use of food stamps, from 26 million people in 2007 to 44 million in 2016.[4] When the election of Donald Trump brought a new emphasis on job creation and retention and the economy started to roar, SNAP enrollment dipped to 39.3 million in 2018. This is still too high for a thriving country with a low unemployment rate. To give this number some perspective, it's more than the entire population of Canada. In our country, during times of high unemployment, states have the power to extend the three-month limit for receiving food stamps; they have the power to revoke the extension as jobs reports improve. But there is a lingering problem when people become "used" to living with benefits such as SNAP and unemployment insurance.

I agree with Louisiana Congressman Garret Graves, who pointed this out as the economy was perking along in summer 2018. "There are talented people across our country who aren't pursuing the full potential of their capabilities, largely because government incentives make it more profitable in some cases to stay home and collect welfare than to pursue personal growth and responsibility through work. Government needs to provide a safety net for the vulnerable, but it's become a lifestyle for some to actively choose government assistance over work."[5]

Disability benefits—which are, of course, another humane program that working folks pay into, like Social Security, to be assured of basic sustenance in case of birth disability, crippling illness, or injury—can also be too liberally administered for anyone's good. In isolated cases, disability entitlements can—and there is evidence that they have—become something of a disincentive to work. The program is designed to aid only workers who become unable to do their jobs—at least temporarily. Those receiving disability benefits are not counted as unemployed. These benefits are widely referred to by the acronym SSDI (Social Security Disability Insurance).

The number of people receiving SSDI has been falling since 2014, and the share of insured workers who take benefits has been falling since 2013. In 2010, about 1 million *new recipients* entered the program. By 2016, that number had plummeted to barely 700,000, and more people were leaving the program than joining. In total, however, the disability rolls grew by more than 1 million people between 2008 and 2016, before the dip that came with economic improvement.[6]

During the recessionary period under the Obama administration, the SSDI program in some regions seemed to emerge as a second, semihidden form of unemployment insurance for those whose jobs had dried up. In 2013, National Public Radio's "Planet Money" program reported, after six months of travel and interviews with people in the program, that the rise in enrollment numbers closely correlated with the areas of the United States where job flight and outsourcing closed plants, mills, and other major employers. Chana Joffe-Walt summarized the situation as follows:

> Disability has also become a de facto welfare program for people without a lot of education or job skills But it wasn't supposed to serve this purpose; it's not a retraining program designed to get people back onto their feet. Once people go onto disability, they almost never go back to work . . . [they] qualify for Medicare, the government healthcare program that also covers the elderly.

They also get disability payments from the government of about $13,000 a year. This isn't great. But if your alternative is a minimum wage job that will pay you at most $15,000 a year, and probably does not include health insurance, disability may be a better option.[7]

Another reporter, Vox.com's Dylan Matthews, recently did his own in-depth investigation into disability. He traveled to high-enrollment counties in Tennessee. What he reported confirms that there are questions about whether going on temporary disability discourages work, but he documents that most recipients truly enroll as a last resort because they are "desperately sick and injured" and cannot work.

Matthews argues that "SSDI is not a gusher of free federal money for lazy people with backaches. It's a stingy, hard-to-access program that helps some of the country's most desperate citizens scrape by; applying takes months or years, and more than 60 percent of applicants wind up being rejected anyway. . . . SSDI is a thin piece of duct tape holding the American safety net together, ensuring people hit with severe medical misfortune have some means of survival."[8]

I encourage you to read both of these articles because they help cut through the confusion about this controversial issue and provide real-life examples of how important is to take care of one's health. My message is this: if you are sick or injured and need to leave the workforce, do everything you possibly can—working with your doctor, occupational and physical therapists, or whomever—to recover. Then *go back to work*. The Newtonian principle of physics also applies to your career: *a body at rest tends to stay at rest; a body in motion tends to stay in motion.*

REAP THE EXTRAORDINARY REWARDS OF WORK

As soon as people come off the sidelines and into the workforce, the benefits begin to flow. Some of these benefits—such as eligibility for Social Security payments—don't show up until later in life. Most of the benefits of work, however, are available to people throughout each stage of their lives. The number one job benefit, of course, is that money flows into your bank account. Anyone who has ever experienced the income spigot being turned off should feel the joy every day when it's turned on. The benefits beyond income that attach to work should be counted daily, too—or maybe weekly, along with the paycheck. They are diverse and super valuable but often underrated.

Job Benefit No. 2: Skills

When you are working, you use your skills. You hone and polish them, and you gain new skills all the time, whether it feels like it or not. Our public education system has been allowed to deteriorate, unfortunately. And that has left us with a skills gap. There are jobs going begging in this country. "The U.S. needs 50,000 truck drivers to avoid a shipping squeeze," the American Trucking Association found in a 2017 report.[9] There is a shortage of nurses and skilled caretakers that will continue to grow as baby boomers grow older (around 10,000 of these "fogies" retire every day, according to the Pew Research Center).[10]

Workers with computer skills are sought after, especially in manufacturing jobs. The Bureau of Labor Statistics projects that there will be a quarter of a million new jobs in computer software created in the decade 2016–2026—jobs paying better than $100,000 per year. There will be 140,000 accountant and auditor jobs paying $70,000 per year, 129,000 medical secretary positions paying $35,000 per year, and 113,000 maintenance and repair jobs paying

$38,000 per year. Scads of new jobs requiring little or no unique skills will also become available, but most are low paying. However, even with a job as a personal care assistant, for instance, paying around $23,000 per year, it is possible to train and become better qualified and earn more (see Figure 6.1).

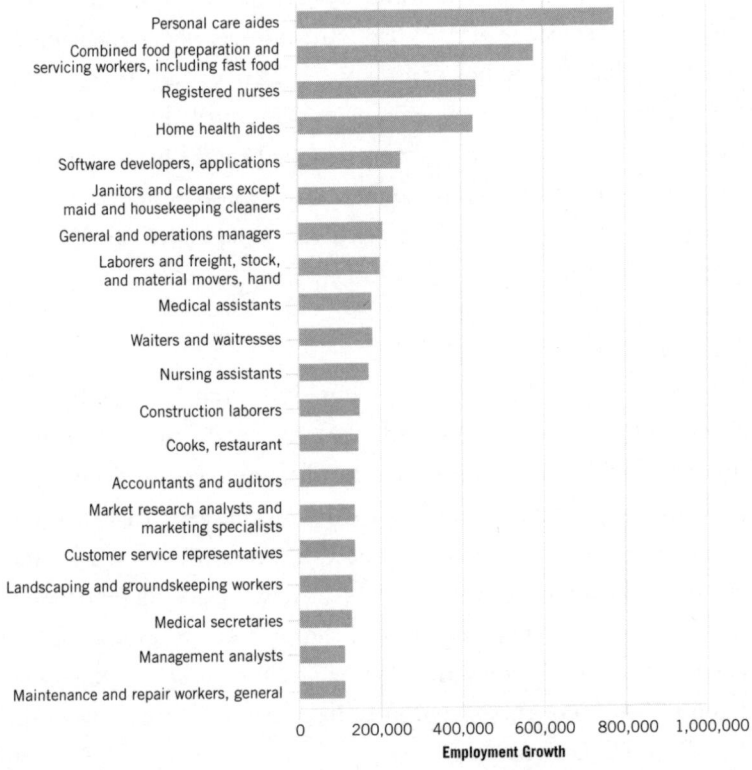

FIGURE 6.1 Most new jobs: employment growth, projected 2016–2026[11]

Any opportunity—and I mean *any*—to add to your portfolio of skills or improve them is valuable in our high-tech job market. Yes, automation is a significant, scary threat to many workers. It is a fact that robots and computers will come for many of the positions filled by hardworking Americans in the past. This is only another vital reason to develop your skills and keep them fresh.

Even the most maligned (and unfair) stereotype of a bad job—flipping burgers at McDonald's—is losing its edge because the company understands that it needs educated, engaged, and eager-to-learn employees who want to move up the career ladder. McDonald's is tripling its investment (to the tune of $150 million) in its Archways to Opportunity tuition-assistance program over the next five years. It also provides free classes in English as a second language and a free accredited online education program for anyone who wants to earn his or her GED (high school graduate equivalence degree). Free training to get the vital skills to grow your bottom line—what's not to like?

Many states began programs during the worst of the Great Recession to try to provide more training for people who were out of work. I am always a little skeptical of government being effective at job training, but these are indeed worth checking out—especially if they are offered for free. How do you check them out? Well, there's Google. If you are unemployed and receiving benefits, pay attention to the lists of referrals your caseworker will provide about training and retraining, and always follow up. If you are interested in training for something specific, be persistent about calling, emailing, and even visiting in person to make an application.

In many areas, business and government are working together to provide accredited courses and internships in science, technology, engineering, and mathematics (STEM)—the most employable skills of the future—starting with people as young as middle school students. San Bernardino County in California has been a hotbed of innovation, training students and plugging them into jobs in manufacturing, shipping, and healthcare. One county program introduces high school students to career opportunities to work in medical offices and hospitals. It permits high school seniors to take a state test to gain medical assistant certificates for entry-level work. "When people think of healthcare careers, they often think of nurses and doctors, but this pilot program exposes high school students to the array of career options in medicine. These are good paying jobs with significant upward mobility," said William Gilbert, who directs the Arrowhead Regional Medical Center, where the teenagers train. "It's rewarding for us to be part of this program to not only educate, but to also help to retain our county's best and brightest young people."[12]

These types of partnerships are flourishing nationwide. As a land grant university, Rutgers, the State University of New Jersey, has partnered with New Jersey's 4-H program for more than 100 years. While developers have long ago paved and built over many of the farms that once earned New Jersey its slogan as the Garden State, 4-H participation is soaring. Students are learning STEM and technical skills and exploring the needs for healthier, afford-able food in every part of the state. "In Essex and Hudson counties, where food deserts have replaced farms, interest in traditional 4-H agriculture-based programs is booming," said Marissa Staffen, a Rutgers' county 4-H agent in Essex County. Student and volunteer participation is high in the multiple community gardens she over-sees in towns such as Montclair, Newark, Jersey City, East Orange, and Kearny. "The hope is that by educating today's urban youth about food systems and their community's food needs, they will have the knowledge to advocate for themselves and their neighbors tomorrow."[13]

STEM training and education partnerships and scholarships are springing up around the nation—search online to see what you can discover in the area where you live.

Job Benefit No. 3: Benefits

One huge benefit of having a full-time job—as opposed to work-ing as an independent contractor—is, well, benefits. For a starter, most jobs offer health insurance benefits. Other benefits might include maternity leave, family medical leave, a 401(k) plan, credit union accounts to save for your kids' education, and free financial counseling. These ancillary benefits of employment are tangible and meaningful, and they are dollar based. They can help in all sorts of situations. While it is possible to get "Obamacare" insurance on your own, it is no piece of cake to navigate the online marketplace and secure the best deal for yourself. If you are insured through your employer, you generally will be given some options for the type of plan that suits you best. You will also receive guidance and assistance in securing the plan and paying for it with automatic deductions from your paycheck.

Even if you have to leave the job or your company goes under, you have the chance to extend the coverage you have chosen for up to 18 months on the Consolidated Omnibus Budget Reconciliation Act (COBRA) plan—don't worry about the bureaucratic gobbledygook. You can continue to pay for health benefits through your employer, although you pay the full value of the premium. This is still likely to be cheaper than purchasing the same insurance in the marketplace.

I won't belabor the point about having the possibility of a 401(k) and other retirement savings plans through your workplace because I'll be going into that in depth in Chapter 7. Every employee should be fully aware that the ability to make tax-free investments of your earnings is a terrific boon.

I always advise those leaving a full-time job for the "gig economy" to give careful consideration before they jump. While I admire the entrepreneurial spirit involved in self-employment and fully understand why people enjoy freelancing at whatever they are good at— many of the side benefits of work are lost with the freelance life. This can have serious and long-term consequences that must be recognized and analyzed financially. Please keep in mind that you must tackle issues that include purchasing health insurance on your own and funding your retirement savings as well as paying quarterly estimated taxes and Social Security taxes.

So whatever you do, make an informed decision.

As a partner at our law firm, I happen to work with a lot of women, and I always advise them to think long and hard before quitting a job when they begin their families. They must carefully weigh the value of employment benefits they receive and think about what the loss of those mean. They also should be aware of the effect a work gap in a résumé may have on future career prospects as some employers do not look kindly on them.

Job Benefit No. 4: Mental Health and Self-Worth

Unless you're fortunate, whatever you do at work and in your career means that you will change jobs. Some people love their job despite having a terrible boss. Union or government jobs can provide security but lull you into taking your career and skills for granted. Others of us have unrealistic views of how "happy" work can make you. Never forget that a job is first a source of income and benefits for you and your family. A job enables you to begin or continue a journey toward a healthy net worth while advancing your skills and experience.

You have options beyond quitting, of course. You can seek a transfer within a company, if it is large enough. You can meet with a job coach and friends you trust to get different perspectives on whether you can improve your job situation before making the final decision to move on. Some terrific books have been published that provide career advice.[14] Read a few before you have a big crisis at work, and be prepared for your next career transition.

My point here is to flip the flashlight on an aspect of a decent job that many take for granted. Work provides a psychological foundation that we tend to forget until it's gone. Work is good for your health; it provides self-esteem, companionship, and a sense of status.

A highly respected 10-year survey by the Society for Human Resources Management showed that between 2005 and 2015, the share of us saying we were modestly or very satisfied in our jobs ranged from a low of only 77 percent to 88 percent.[15] Other figures are stark: long-term unemployment is associated with depression, anxiety, and even increasing rates of suicide. Studies show work gives us social contacts, social status, and a sense of identity and personal achievement. You can make lifelong friends and even find love.

Taking on a job change or promotion and succeeding provide an enormous and permanent boost to one's self-confidence and self-esteem. One group of psychiatrists found that "[t]he potential positive effects of good work and the role work can play in facilitating recovery from an illness and enhancing mental well-being need to be highlighted and promoted more widely."[16]

I've been pleasantly surprised at the self-worth and satisfaction I have experienced as a law partner at a big law firm. As I built a law practice with my team, I found it rewarding to help our clients through difficult times and challenges. I've worked in the hedge fund business for 10 years, the Securities and Exchange Commission for five years, wrote a book for one year, and am now at Kirkland & Ellis. At this point, I have seen nearly every variation of every issue under the federal securities laws somewhere before. Now I get to deploy all that knowledge to help my clients.

I know that I am a lucky man; the unexpected icing is using all I've done in my career to help people who are in a tough way. I often tell the young lawyers on my team that legal skills can open many doors to helping people over the course of their careers. They may not yet hear it with all the deadlines we give them, but they will, they will.

Job Benefit No. 5: Social Security

Social Security is the foundation of retirement security and a great poverty fighter. However, you aren't entitled to your benefits without working. Your time on the job is critical to the size of your Social Security retirement benefit.

You need to work at least 10 years to become eligible for Social Security. The Social Security Administration (SSA) has a system of credits. Every year you earn four credits, and you need a total of 40 credits to qualify. The years you take off from work can affect the size of your benefits. The SSA bases your retirement benefit on your highest 35 years of earnings and your age when you start receiving benefits.

Many women don't realize that their Social Security checks are going to be smaller (if they're not receiving benefits through a spouse) if they don't put in the time and move up in the workforce. If you're divorced but were married for at least 10 years—and haven't remarried—you're eligible to claim Social Security under your ex-spouse's earnings if they turn out to be higher than your own.

Whatever you do, don't blow off thinking about Social Security because you've heard or read the common trope that the fund is going to run out of money. Congress will not stop worrying about the votes of 120 million people. Social Security will almost certainly be available for your retirement no matter how young you are. The stakes are just too high for anything else to happen, barring a zombie apocalypse. The many challenging issues of financing Social Security will result at worst in a slight diminution of benefits or an increase in the retirement age for full benefits.

Social Security benefits work with your tax-protected retirement savings and other income (real estate income, for example) to provide a guaranteed predictable income stream. The details of Social Security retirement benefits tend to be misunderstood even by financial types because they seem so far off in the future. Here is a list of essential facts as of 2019 about how the program works and who it helps:

- Social Security provided benefits to nearly 61 million Americans in 2017. Among beneficiaries aged 65 and older, one-fifth of married couples and four in 10 unmarried people rely on benefits for 90 percent or more of their income. About half of married couples and 70 percent of single persons get at least half their income from Social Security.

- You can start receiving retirement benefits at age 62, but your check will be bigger if you wait until your SSA-designated full retirement age or later. (Full retirement age is 66 for those born between 1943 and 1954. It then gradually increases each year until it reaches 67 for those born in 1960 and later.) The longer you wait to start collecting, the higher is the amount you will receive. By delaying Social Security beyond your full retirement age, your benefit will go up 8 percent a year until you reach age 70.
- The SSA bases your benefits on the earnings on which you paid Social Security payroll taxes. The higher your earnings (up to a maximum taxable amount of $132,900 in 2019), the higher is your benefit.
- Without Social Security benefits, about 40 percent of retired Americans would have incomes below the poverty line, assuming that other social conditions remain equal, according to official estimates. Social Security benefits lift more than 15 million elderly Americans out of poverty.[17]
- Once you start receiving Social Security checks, your benefits will increase to keep pace with inflation, helping to ensure that people do not fall into poverty as they age.[18]

Social Security benefits are most helpful to low- and moderate-income retirees who have had fewer resources to save for retirement. Of course, many people of modest means still do a great job of saving. Social Security is also of disproportionate importance to women, statistically speaking, because they tend to live longer. Anyone who receives the benefit has paid into it, so each of us can feel that we have a stake.

CONCLUSION

Thank goodness the Social Security safety net will be there. But I also want more for you and for everyone who's working and building a career of whatever kind. I want you to make the most of your experiences and skills to increase your earnings and find job satisfaction. "Social mobility" is a way of expressing the American dream of building wealth and improving your way of life by pursuing your ambitions. Do not be taken in by the demagogues who say that vast disparities of wealth in America have dented the American dream because the system is "rigged." Opportunities are there for all Americans for the taking—and the path always begins with a job.

In the years after the Great Recession, social mobility slowed down, which is natural after a downturn. But it is still very possible and real. Use your job to network, meet new people, and find out where your skills are needed. Take advantage of tuition and training opportunities your employer offers so that you can tackle a promotion. Join a professional or trade organization. Go to the company picnic.

Jobs aren't just paychecks. They're engines of opportunity. If you want to survive the next crisis, if you want to prosper, if you want better for your family, a job puts you in a much better spot to achieve those dreams.

Saving Your Way to a Better Life

CHAPTER 7

Money is a terrible master, but an excellent servant.

—P. T. BARNUM

Thank you so much for reading this far. I genuinely believe that you are on your way to finding more happiness by using these simple strategies to reduce the fear and stress that can take away the joy of living. What we experience in this life of ours makes it hard to get our priorities straight. The media blasts us with political controversy, noise, and finger pointing. We are distracted by disturbing news stories of crime, scandal, and abuse. Everything is magnified. Sports scandals! Buy a lottery ticket! Deadly storms! Stream a new Netflix show every day! All the while the vast majority of us are still busy as heck. We're going to work, taking care of our families, walking the dog, checking homework, stopping in on Grandma at the assisted-living place, finding the right summer camps, buying a birthday gift for our niece, and on and on. Not to mention, there's the fun side of life, whether you're dating, seeing friends, going to the farmers' market, or hitting the beach.

In the midst of this noise and distraction, the media and politicians and experts lost interest in addressing the basics of managing money. I structured this book to show how fundamental the math is: stop your outgo (Part 1), increase your income (Part 2), and build your savings and investments for the long term (Part 3). You need a safety net and a secure strategy for your later years.

The math is easy, but I recognize that life can still be hard and unfair.

The Great Recession of the 2008 period tore deeply into the fabric of families and communities. Employers laid off 15 million workers between 2007 and 2010. The unemployment rate doubled during that period and was the highest since 1982. More than 7 in 10 Americans were personally affected by the recession, according to surveys conducted by the Heldrich Center for Workforce Development at Rutgers University in 2014: in fact, 23 percent of us lost a job during the recession, 11 percent knew someone in their immediate household who lost a job, 26 percent knew someone in their extended family who was laid off, and 13 percent had a close personal friend who was laid off.[1]

Perhaps your mom or dad, sister or brother was laid off. This hardship could have affected your family life or education. Maybe you occupied Wall Street or cheered on those who did. The recession's impact, the sizes of the federal bailouts, and 24/7 news coverage made many of us cynical and distrustful. It seemed to many of us then that capitalism could do no good. For others, capitalism can do no wrong. The truth is somewhere in between. Capitalism creates jobs and destroys them. This is the "creative destruction" of Joseph Schumpeter that allows our economy to grow and regenerate as it adjusts to innovation and change. The key is that you are not a boat tossed helplessly on the waves. You can use planning and common sense to maximize the good times and minimize the bad. When it comes to your money, the federal government passed laws that protect your savings and make your retirement savings tax free.

SAVINGS IS THE KEY

So the Great Recession scared us and dried up some of the easy money that got us into debt. For millions, though, our personal savings rate hasn't been enough to put aside a nest egg for tough times and save for retirement. And we lag way behind other advanced nations in our savings rates.

Too many of us are still making bad decisions about what to do with the cash we have. We can be lured by overhyped investing pitches and affinity fraud schemes that suggest becoming rich through esoteric strategies usually involving going into more debt and taking on more risk. My view is that when you're in a hole, don't trust the person who gives you a bigger shovel.

The Federal Reserve's report on economic well-being in 2018 shows that Americans have been feeling and doing better financially since 2013. But Americans are still struggling mightily with savings. Four in 10 adults lack the money to cover an unexpected $400 expense, and even fewer say that they are on track with their retirement savings.[2]

The e-commerce consumer-oriented site for financial services ValuePenguin crunched the data from the Federal Reserve's 2016 gold standard survey of American saving rates and confirmed that huge swaths of our population lack adequate savings:

- Households with incomes between $45,000 and $70,000 have a median savings of $2,500; for households earning between $25,000 and $45,000, the median savings is only $1,400. (ValuePenguin measures with a median, which is more accurate than averages, which skew the number upward as a result of a relative handful of big savers at the top of the distribution.)
- Robustly middle-class households with incomes between $70,000 and $115,000 reported median savings of $6,000.
- Male-headed households had median savings of $9,200, whereas female-headed households reported median savings of $2,500, which reflects the more tenuous economics of female-earner households.[3]

We can't forget the devastation of 2008 nor that we will have downturns in the future.

But we have to open our eyes. We have to remember that our best choice is to prepare for the worst. "The time to repair the roof is when the sun is shining," President John Kennedy once said of economic policy, and this remains true. It's time to repair the roof on your financial house. A job helps keep out the rain, but nothing keeps you dry like savings.

To be sure, a savings "roof" only goes so far, and if you are unemployed, don't like your job, or want or need to make better money, you will have to meet those challenges as well. Three-quarters of the unemployed find jobs in less than six months, the government's figures show.[4] Therefore, a six-month nest egg will cover the needs of a sizable majority of the unemployed. But a savings strategy encompasses even more to provide a financial roof over your head.

My savings roof has four pillars:

1. Saving cash equal to six months of your monthly living costs
2. Paying down high-interest credit-card debt
3. Beginning a tax-protected retirement fund
4. Opening additional savings accounts for your priorities, such as higher education savings for your kids or, for adult earners, courses, degrees, and certificates to continue building and finding new skills.

PILLAR NO. 1: THE SIX-MONTH CUSHION

Make cash savings and paying off high-interest credit-card debt your first two priorities. If you have more than $500 in high-interest credit-card debt, start paying that off each month. However, you also need to build the savings habit, so create a separate savings account with small automatic withdrawals from each paycheck. Do this even if you're saving no more than $25 per month. A savings reserve equal to six months of your monthly living costs also protects you from high-interest credit-card debt. People often use credit cards for unexpected expenses, and many credit-card horror stories could be avoided by saving a sufficient amount in an emergency fund.

Every single financial writer in history, it would be safe to surmise, recommends having your bank deduct savings from your paycheck or checking account. Most banks will deduct a certain amount from your checking account into an interest-bearing savings account. Some larger institutions offer savings vehicles that add 25 cents or the like every time you use your debit card. However, as I will explain shortly, savings accounts linked digitally to checking accounts are quite inviting to raid. If you want to explore, some apps and online accounts specialize in helping you save (learn more at the Money Under Thirty blog):

- The Digit.co app analyzes your checking account and makes small deductions that you don't notice and won't interfere with paying bills. You must, however, use one of Digit's partner banks. As of this writing, the app bills you $2.99 a month, so if you aren't finding that Digit saves more money than you would through a standard payroll deduction, cancel it.
- Capital One's online 360 "bank" offers savings accounts that are super transparent and user friendly. You can create as many 25 different accounts under one login with no fees. This option empowers you to establish multiple savings buckets for different needs—vacation, education, emergency fund, holiday shopping, and so forth. (Remember, the emergency fund comes first!) Other online banks, including Ally and Alliant, offer similar services.
- If you are an iPhone user, the Money Clouds app does the savings bucket thing in an Apple way. The app generates various cloud savings accounts in partnership with a

participating bank and tracks data from your bank account as you make progress toward a goal.

In the case of these newer apps, check the fine print to be sure that there are no excessive or hidden fees. All these tools can be helpful, but they won't matter unless you commit to building your personal balance sheet by

1. Reducing the outflow
2. Increasing the inflow until income exceeds expenses (you have a personal profit)
3. Setting that profit aside for savings

A significant share of America's citizens lack access to neighborhood banks. They may have limited mobility or need to take a bus or taxi to reach a bank branch office far from their homes. Payday loan offices tend to set up shop in just these neighborhoods, where they are attractive to the vulnerable. While these lenders can provide short-term help, it is far better to have your own savings account to get you through rough times. Neither you nor I would enjoy or feel comfortable having to travel an hour to use a bank. This lack of access is true not only in urban areas but also in rural areas. The online savings programs mentioned earlier are a perfect solution for those who find themselves in this situation. Many banks also offer no-fee essential banking services that can help you set up accounts.

Just a couple of generations ago, savings accounts were available at the U.S. Post Office. In the twenty-first century, I would not support bringing banking services to that inefficient location. However, just as the internet has drastically reduced post office visits, it can also provide access to savings accounts for millions.

Nearly one-third of Americans live within 1 mile of where they went to high school, and more than half live within 10 miles, according to a Federal Reserve report on economic well-being.[5] To some degree, geography is destiny, and getting loans from a payday shop is going to happen where that is the only game in the neighborhood.

The same report found that people, particularly older Americans, still want local banks.

More than 6 in 10 Americans rate having a neighborhood bank or credit union as moderately or very important. This ratio jumps to 68 percent for those between the ages of 50 and 59 years and to 72 percent for those over age 60. Having more people in the habit of saving is so paramount to our economic present and future that we need to address it on a neighborhood-by-neighborhood basis.

Heavy-handed postcrisis regulation of banks caused the number of new banks started in the United States to drop to zero. In late 2018, even U.S. Senator Elizabeth Warren advocated for decreased regulation of community banks. Let's get regulators to encourage the formation and expansion of banks, not discourage it. If people save, banks will come calling to neighborhoods to provide services. That's how free markets work.

PILLAR NO. 2: ELIMINATE CREDIT-CARD DEBT

As part of your budget, you'll need to set aside cash to pay off your credit-card debt. You've probably seen ads and received pitches for cards offering a "balance transfer" that allows you to switch your credit-card balances to a new piece of plastic that provides a reduced interest rate (often 0 percent) for an introductory period of around 12 to 18 months. During this period, you can focus on paying off the principal without accruing interest.

Transferring your balance generally has a fee (around 3 percent of the balance), but it's usually quite small compared with the alternative—a year's worth of compounding interest at high rates. For balance transfers to work, you need a plan to pay off the debt during the no-interest introductory period. Such offers don't automatically make your debt disappear, but they can help you tackle it a bit more comfortably.[6]

As I've written earlier in this book, these offers aren't designed to serve you the consumer. They're meant to make you a new customer, and if you end up not paying off the debt and paying higher interest again, that's money in the credit-card issuer's pocket. Balance transfers can be a lot like the excellent professor who gave you an extension on your term paper: you get some breathing room, but if you don't finish the job, you'll still fail the class. It's important to understand the terms of your balance transfer. Some cards will charge you back interest as if the promo period never happened if you miss a payment or don't pay off the balance by the end of the period.

Other Strategies

1. If you have debt on multiple cards, you can aggressively pay off the one with the highest interest rate first. This saves money in the long run. By contrast, some people prefer to tackle the smallest balance first—this can provide a psychological boost in the form of a quick victory. Studies by Remi Trudel of the Questrom School of Business at Boston College confirm this.[7] With both strategies, it's important to pay more than the minimum for the balance you're trying to eliminate.
2. Ask the credit-card companies to reduce their interest rates. This request is more likely to work if you have a better credit history and a healthy relationship with this particular company.
3. A personal loan through your bank can offer a more favorable interest rate than your credit card and save you money in the long run (e.g., taking out a $20,000 loan at 10 percent to pay off your $20,000 credit-card balance with a 25 percent interest rate). This only works if you use the loan exclusively to pay off the credit-card debt—and don't add more to it.

PILLAR NO. 3: UNCLE SAM IS GIVING YOU FREE MONEY. WHY ARE YOU TURNING IT DOWN?

If you are employed and you have not signed up for putting deductions from your paycheck into your company's tax-protected retirement plans, usually Individual Retirement Accounts (IRAs) or 401(k)s, do it now. A range of retirement savings plans exists. Table 7.1 provides an explanation of what each one is.

TABLE 7.1 Retirement Savings Plans

401(k) Plan	This is a defined contribution plan where an employee can make contributions from his or her paycheck either before or after-tax, depending on the options offered in the plan. In some plans, the employer also makes contributions such as matching the employee's contributions up to a certain percentage. SIMPLE and safe harbor 401(k) plans have mandatory employer contributions.
403(b) Tax-Sheltered Annuity (TSA) Plans	This is a retirement plan offered by public schools and certain tax-exempt organizations. An individual's 403(b) annuity can be obtained only under an employer's TSA plan. Generally, these annuities are funded by elective deferrals made under salary reduction agreements and nonelective employer contributions.
Annuity	A series of payments under a contract that are made at regular intervals and over a period of more than one year.
Defined Benefit Plan	Also known as a traditional pension plan, a db plan promises the participant a specified monthly benefit at retirement. Often, the benefit is based on factors such as the participant's salary, age, and the number of years he or she worked for the employer. The plan may state this promised benefit as an exact dollar amount, such as $100 per month at retirement. Or, more commonly, it may calculate a benefit through a plan formula that considers such factors as salary and service.

(continued on next page)

TABLE 7.1 Retirement Savings Plans (*continued*)

Defined Contribution Plan	This is a retirement plan in which the employee and/or the employer contribute to the employee's individual account under the plan. The amount in the account at distribution includes the contributions and investment gains or losses, minus any investment and administrative fees. Generally, the contributions and earnings are not taxed until distribution. The value of the account will change based on contributions and the value and performance of the investments. Examples of defined contribution plans include 401(k) plans, 403(b) plans, employee stock ownership plans, and profit-sharing plans.
Savings Incentive Match Plan for Employees of Small Employers (SIMPLE)	A plan in which a business with 100 or fewer employees can offer retirement benefits through employee salary reductions and employer nonelective or matching contributions (similar to those found in a 401(k) plan). It can be either a SIMPLE IRA or a SIMPLE 401(k). SIMPLE IRA plans impose few administrative burdens on employers because IRAs are owned by the employees, and the bank or financial institution receiving the funds does most of the paperwork. While each has some different features, including contribution limits and the availability of loans, required employer contributions are immediately 100 percent vested in both.
Simplified Employee Pension Plan (SEP)	A plan in which an employer contributes on a tax-favored basis to IRAs owned by its employees. If the employer meets certain conditions, it isn't subject to the reporting and disclosure requirements of most retirement plans.

This change is the single most powerful step you can take to strengthen your balance sheet. First, this is automatic savings. Second, it is coming out of your paycheck before taxes, so it reduces your taxable income, thus reducing the overall tax you have to pay. Third, you're salting money away where no one can touch it. (In Chapter 8, I'll provide a ton of specific guidance for getting the most out of your savings.)

Whether you're a Democrat, Republican, Libertarian, or Independent, would you tear up about a check sent to you from the federal government? I didn't think so. What if your employer wants to give you a raise? Would you turn it down? Of course not. Well,

many employers match your contribution to your 401(k) with addi-
tional money you wouldn't receive any other way. This is one of the
greatest deals in the modern world, so sign up for your 401(k) or
IRA today.

About 6 in 10 of us are offered a retirement contribution by
our employers (excluding the federal government and household
employees), and the participating rate among those eligible is about
7 in 10. The rate should be much higher.[8] Many employers now
automatically enroll employees in their retirement plans with the
choice to opt out rather than filling out a form to opt in. This is a
really great innovation, and you should encourage your employer to
explore it.

Among 401(k) plans offered by Vanguard, for example, the
participation rate is 90 percent when employees are automatically
enrolled (with the choice to opt out), 63 percent for nonautomatic
(i.e., opt-in) enrollment. This discrepancy is particularly steep with
employees 25 years of age and younger: only 27 percent participate
with voluntary enrollment as opposed to 85 percent with automatic
enrollment plans.[9] And according to a 2017 national survey conducted by the respected think tank the Employee Benefit Research
Institute, "roughly two-thirds of employed workers who are not currently saving for retirement would be likely to save if their employer
made automatic deductions [from their paycheck] into a savings
account."[10] Think about what this tells you.

Some employers have a waiting period before they enroll you
that lasts from three to six months to at most a year. During the
waiting period, you can open a traditional IRA and start contribut-
ing your pretax dollars. As long as you are employed, you can contribute pretax dollars to a traditional IRA. As of 2019, the Internal
Revenue Service (IRS) limit for annual contributions is $6,000. If
you are over 50 years old, the IRS allows you to contribute more to
your retirement account—an additional $1,000 per year more than
is allowed for workers under age 50—to help you "catch up."

I know that it is hard to set aside money from a paycheck that you surely could spend, but remind yourself, "it's my money." This is your mantra. I never think of my IRA and 401(k) savings as retirement money at all. I think of them as part of my net worth. When I speak of building your personal balance sheet, consider tax-free accounts the single best way to bolster that balance sheet.

There are many ways your retirement accounts can make you wealthier. First, they add to your net worth and financial confidence. Second, in certain circumstances, you can borrow against these funds—but as a next-to-last resort. Third, if you get in real trouble, you can withdraw from them and pay a penalty tax. You should only consider this as a true last resort with no other options. You indeed will feel the tax bite.

PILLAR NO. 4: THE TRUE MEANING OF SAVINGS

Wherever and whenever you experience those ineffable moments that give you the greatest joy—the money you saved (or your parents or grandparents saved) likely made those possible: the pride of seeing your daughter or son walk across the stage on her or his college graduation day; the day you moved into your first house; the joy of seeing your children open their presents on Christmas or Hannukah; the delight of the new car you bought for you and your spouse after your last child graduated from college because you had some savings left over; the giddy fun you had with your friends on a special long golf trip you saved for over the years. Whatever it may be.

Savings are the primary vehicle that Americans use to achieve their goals. Savings open the way to education, upward mobility, and better opportunities for our kids. After you have your emergency fund and retirement accounts purring along, you can begin to save for your lifetime goals, whatever those might be.

Perhaps you're ready to save for higher education. If so, you can take advantage of 529 plans, which allow you to enjoy tax breaks while saving for college. States regulate 529 plans. Each state has its own wrinkles in how it "does" 529s. Some 529s offer a "prepaid tuition program," which means that you use your savings to purchase tuition credits at participating colleges and universities for *future* tuition fees at *current* prices. Prepaid tuition plans typically can't be used to pay for room and board or tuition for elementary and secondary schools. Most prepaid tuition plans have residency requirements. I advise extreme caution when considering a prepaid program. Examine the fine print and details in your state. Your savings are earmarked for in-state schools.

The second type of 529 plan is not as restrictive and far more popular. Education savings plans let you save for tuition, mandatory fees, *and* room and board. Withdrawals can generally be used at any college or university, sometimes including non-U.S. colleges and universities. Education savings plans can also be used to pay up to $10,000 per year per beneficiary for tuition at any public, private, or religious elementary or secondary school. Most of these 529 plans do not require that you live in that state.

States choose the investment managers for their 529 programs. For example, New York state uses Vanguard; New Jersey uses Franklin Templeton. You want the manager to be one of the major low- or no-fee families of mutual funds. Typically, states offer age-based portfolios, which shift their investing allocation toward more conservative investments as the beneficiary gets closer to college age. If you are using a 529 account to pay for elementary or secondary school tuition, you may have a shorter time horizon for your money to grow. You also may not feel comfortable taking on riskier or more volatile investments if you plan on withdrawing the money soon.

All education savings plans are sponsored by state governments, but only a few have residency requirements for the saver and/or beneficiary. Education savings plan investments in mutual funds and exchange-traded funds (ETFs) are not federally guaranteed, but investments in some principal-protected bank products may be insured by the Federal Deposit Insurance Corporation. As with most investments, your education savings plan accounts are not guaranteed and could lose some or all of the money invested.

Best of all, if you use your 529 fund for its intended purpose, your earnings are not subject to federal income tax or, in many cases, state income tax. Again, each state's program has to be researched in depth. Don't think 529s are solely for long-term saving for a child's education. Adult earners and learners can also use 529s for community college courses and professional certifications as long as they are participating institutions.

Some of you may not need to save for any further education and are keeping pace with your retirement investing needs. Then by all means open an account with automatic contributions (that you can afford) for other goals you have: a "bucket list" trip, a country cottage, a new violin, or a bamboo fishing rod.

The Inheritance Maze

And then there's this: when you inherit money from your parents or others, you will be challenged as to what to do with the funds. An average of one in five Americans gets some inheritance or wealth transfer, according to an eight-year study by the U.S. Bureau of Labor Statistics.[11] This isn't a large number, but inheritance issues present an often overlooked challenge in a lifetime of dealing with our money issues. Keep in mind that owing to changes in the tax code, federal estate taxes only apply to estates above a very high threshold ($5.6 million for 2018), and some states levy estate taxes of their own. The estate pays estate taxes before distributing assets (the inheritance) to the beneficiary. Other tax situations will vary depending on your state and the type of inheritance you're receiving. TurboTax.com offers a good overview of how to reduce your estate tax burden.

It's tempting to spend an inheritance quickly because it can come unexpectedly and often in a time of grief. Large sums of unexpected money provide a bolt of endorphins and excitement than can overwhelm even the most financially cautious. One study done in Denmark found that, on average, people blow through their inheritance within five years.[12] It is easy to overextend oneself without thinking long term, even if you are looking to reinvest Grandma's windfall. For example, if you use a bequest for a down payment on a bigger house, that creates new costs (higher taxes, insurance, and utilities) that can snowball while your income stays the same.

Based on my experience and the advice of many experts I've known, I will provide a couple of suggestions for being smart with any unexpected financial boon:

- Use the money to fund an emergency account.
- Pay off high-interest debt.

Heirs often don't know the size or nature of their inheritance, which can present problems for financial planning. Try to be communicative about this, even if discussing money can be a bit awkward. Meeting with a personal financial planner can forge a bridge between parents and children for financial planning.[13]

To be sure, most of us aren't in the position to receive a large inheritance, if any at all. However, my experience highlights other money problems that can arise for us over the course of our lives. After your parents retire, have an informal meeting about their plans and paperwork. As noted in a Marketwatch.com essay, "ask where your parents' financial records are kept so [that] you can access them if the need arises and keep their retirement income secure. Your questions can serve as a springboard to a larger discussion about their financial situation."

Remember that you can't inherit your parents' debt unless you take possession of an asset such as a home that still carries a mortgage. Their estate is responsible for unpaid medical bills, property, and income taxes—and that reduces the amount of any inheritance.

One insidious form of identity theft occurs where a parent uses his or her (minor or adult) child's data to open credit accounts, which often results in destroyed credit. If this happens, you can try to resolve it with credit-card companies and the credit reporting agencies or even report the fraud to authorities. As I'll show later in this book, you can rebuild your stolen credit by opening a new credit card and making small payments in full each month. Always be extremely careful about cosigning loans with parents or family members. Ask yourself: am I willing to sacrifice my relationship if my family member does not repay this loan? Because that is often the consequence.

The Nest Egg Principle

In one of the great comedies of the 1980s, Albert Brooks's *Lost in America*, a married couple we called "yuppies" at the time decide to "drop out" and tour America. When the Julie Hagerty character, Linda, loses their life savings at a casino, Brooks's "nest egg" rant ("The egg is a protector, like a god, and we sit under the nest egg . . . and we are protected by it. Without it? No protection!") is a classic. You may want to watch the film for that episode alone.

Unfortunately, scammers and low-life investing con artists who feed off investor interest in what the Securities and Exchange Commission (SEC) calls "opaque private markets" are running amok and pose a particular danger to the nest eggs of retirees, the elderly, and the poor. In July 2018, the *Wall Street Journal* reported on a disgusting fraud scheme that combined both affinity and pension stream fraud. (Utah legal firm Ray, Quinney, and Nebeker represent many victims of affinity fraud common in the heavily Mormon communities of the state, and the firm's blog reports on many interesting cases.)

A convicted felon operating out of a strip mall in Nevada was selling a private pension product to retirees through an affinity-group advisory firm called Live Abundant that also sold products from dubious operations. According to Jeanne Eaglesham's fascinating account in the *Wall Street Journal,*

> Scott Kohn, a 64-year-old felon, ran a company from a Nevada strip-mall mailbox that investors claim took them for more than $100 million in losses.
>
> Mr. Kohn's company, Future Income Payments, appears shut, according to court filings. His investors are likely to be wiped out, according to lawyers representing them, who plan to sue scores of firms that sold Future Income products as soon as this week. At least 25 states have taken enforcement actions or are investigating the company.
>
> The blow-up shines a light on the boom in opaque private markets, to which investors have flocked in the hope of doing better than they can in traditional stock and bond markets. Future Income essentially sold investors other people's pensions. Mr. Kohn's firm would find workers entitled to pension payments and temporarily buy the rights to those payments— effectively lending the beneficiaries money against their future pension income in what is called a "pension advance." Then, Future Income would sell the rights to investors for a lump sum.[14]

Many honest and hardworking citizens of Utah have lost much of their retirement savings in this all-too-common crime.

Affinity Fraud in Brief

Affinity fraud involves investment scams associated with a trusted community, ethnic, or religious group. Typically, prominent leaders of the group are unwittingly conned into promoting the investments through their extended networks. Many affinity schemes use Ponzi or pyramid schemes. The SEC lists numerous recent examples of "busts" or enforcements that read like episodes from *Better Call Saul:*[15]

- A Provo, Utah, affinity fraud involved a Ponzi scheme orchestrated by a financial planner targeting members of his church, family, and friends.
- A Chicago-area former Marine masqueraded as a hedge fund trader to defraud fellow veterans, current military members, and other investors in his affinity network.
- The SEC busted a Texas day trader targeting Houston-area Lebanese and Druze communities with a high-frequency trading scheme based on fake brokerage records.
- One hustler used a Ponzi scheme to sell fraudulent promissory notes to African-American investors. The scoundrel promised phony interest rates of 12 to 20 percent and said that the funds would be used to purchase and support small community businesses, such as a laundry, juice bar, or gas station. Incredibly, he also pitched a "sweepstakes" machine that would generate returns of more than 300 percent in the first year.
- The owners of a tiny voice-over-internet video services company stole $6 million from nearly 80 evangelical Christians through fraudulent stock and promissory notes.
- The Los Angeles Persian-Jewish community was fleeced by one of their own, who raised funds from 11 investors and used nearly $1.6 million of investor funds to buy jewelry, high-end cars, and VIP tickets to sporting events. He hosed his friends with promises of exorbitant returns in purported pre–initial public offering shares of well-known companies.

Excerpts from SEC Advisory on Affinity Fraud

Affinity fraud refers to investment scams that prey upon members of identifiable groups, such as religious or ethnic communities, the elderly, or professional groups. The fraudsters who promote affinity scams frequently are—or pretend to be—members of the group. They often enlist respected community or religious leaders from within the group to spread the word about the scheme by convincing those people that a fraudulent investment is legitimate and worthwhile. Many times, those leaders become unwitting victims of the fraudster's ruse.

These scams exploit the trust and friendship that exist in groups of people who have something in common. Because of the tight-knit structure of many groups, it can be difficult for regulators or law enforcement officials to detect an affinity scam. Victims often fail to notify authorities or pursue their legal remedies and instead try to work things out within the group. This is particularly true where the fraudsters have used respected community or religious leaders to convince others to join the investment.

Many affinity scams involve "Ponzi" or pyramid schemes, where new investor money is used to make payments to earlier investors to give the false illusion that the investment is successful. This ploy is used to trick new investors to invest in the scheme and to lull existing investors into believing their investments are safe and secure. In reality, the fraudster almost always steals investor money for personal use. Both types of schemes depend on an unending supply of new investors—when the inevitable occurs and the supply of investors dries up, the whole scheme collapses and investors discover that most or all of their money is gone.[16]

You can read more about affinity fraud at the SEC website. Be aware of the psychological buttons all these affinity schemes are pushing—the notion of *INCOME NOW!* that you will need later can be as hard to resist as that half gallon of mint chocolate chip ice cream in the freezer on a hot summer's night that you're saving for the weekend. *YUM!*

It is not the easiest approach, but this will work—don't put yourself to the test. If an investment sounds too good to be true, it always is. Invest with federally regulated and registered fund managers and brokers. Don't take the pitch on the scheme (or eat the ice cream before the weekend). Life is to be enjoyed, of course, but the pleasures of deferred enjoyment can be all the sweeter.

At the beginning of this chapter, I talked about how little we hear about financial literacy from our media, our leaders, and even our schools amid the hubbub of the information society. We can blame our poor savings habits on all this distraction. But we can do something about it. Start with one hour a week. Take an hour break from scrolling through your social media, and research the ideas discussed in this chapter. Boredom can be good because it makes us face reality, including financial reality. For French existentialist Jean-Paul Sartre, hell was other people. In twenty-first-century advanced democracies, hell may be not having your smartphone when you are alone. What I've shown here is that setting up a savings safety net is simple, short, and low maintenance. But it does require for a short while that you do our homework, run the numbers, and start your journey to a better life.

INVESTING FOR THE FUTURE

Now that you have cut your expenses, increased your income, and paid down debt, it's time to look at how you invest your savings for the future.

Investing Tax Free   8

Two-thirds of professionally managed funds are regularly outperformed by a broad capitalization-weighted index fund with equivalent risk, and those that do appear to produce excess returns in one period are not likely to do so in the next. The record of professionals does not suggest that sufficient predictability exists in the stock market to produce exploitable arbitrage opportunities.

—BURTON G. MALKIEL, *A Random Walk Down Wall Street: The Time-Tested Strategy for Successful Investing*

You are ready. This is the time to begin with safe investment strategies. It does not have to be complicated. Honestly, it doesn't require a great deal of skill. It does require self-discipline, but you have acquired positive habits by now. If you can summon the discipline to "go long" with your investments, you will be astounded at how well that will work for you when it is time to retire. The rate at which investments can compound is almost (I have to say it) *magical.*

Don't believe in magic? In this case, you should. Master a few simple tricks, and the investment income that will be available to you when you are ready to retire will surprise and delight you. Seriously now, the strategies I outline in this chapter provide tried-and-true methods for strong results. Nothing is guaranteed in life or with investing, but history, statistics, economic trend analysis—all that—go into these recommended strategies for wise investment in your future.

How to begin? For anyone, no matter your age, the first step is to take advantage of any tax-free retirement investment opportunities that you have at work. Employer-sponsored retirement savings plans such as a 401(k) are usually a far better deal than many people realize. As I have written previously, many employers match a portion of your contributions to your retirement accounts. Yet, according to many sources, including a 2015 report by the investment advisory firm Financial Engines, 25 percent of Americans don't take full advantage of employee retirement accounts when they have access to them.[1] So make sure that you check this out first, and then stay focused to gain as much as possible.

By contrast, if you don't have a matching plan—and many smaller businesses do not even offer 401(k) plans—you need to begin investing your money anyway. You can participate in tax-protected retirement savings accounts such as IRAs. This can provide some free money too, because you are able to take advantage of one of the rare instances when the federal government will not tax your income as long as it is tucked away in that retirement account. Yes, you will pay taxes when you withdraw the money in your later years, but likely at a lower rate than you would during peak earning years, because your annual retirement income will be less. Your tax bite depends on your total income, your deductions, and your tax bracket for that year. For example, in a year where you have more deductions than income (such as a year with a lot of medical expenses), then you may not pay taxes on withdrawals for that year. And when you retire, some of the magic comes into play, counteracting whatever withdrawal fees you owe. This is the magic of time and compounded interest. The money you are not paying in taxes over the years is certain to grow—maybe not as miraculously fast as Jack's beanstalk, but grow it will.

As an alternative, you can use a Roth IRA to invest with no tax on gains. Under a Roth IRA, you contribute *posttax* money, your investments grow tax free, and you don't pay tax at withdrawal.

There are pros and cons to both types of IRAs, so it is probably best to have some of each.

As you form your investment plan, you will need to think about different ways to invest your money. You might set up a personal investment plan to back up your employee retirement account or your IRA or to serve as your primary retirement savings. Diversification should be a part of your investment strategy, if you can possibly do it. Again, it's not too complicated or skill intensive. I can walk you through a step-by-step guide to starting and managing your investment accounts. In this chapter, I will outline:

- How to save when your employer does not offer a plan
- Types of investment funds and the relative risks of each
- Asset allocation—division of your investment dollars into accounts with different risks and investing goals
- How to evaluate and participate in mutual funds
- Various types of mutual funds and their risk levels—index, global, tax protected, and growth
- Recommendations of top fund management companies with decades of sterling performance and reputation
- More advanced opportunities, such as managing your own stock accounts and investing in real estate

LOOK AT THE HORIZON

Let us begin with the assumption that you are investing with your eventual retirement in mind. No matter what stage of life you are in when you actually start investing, the number one goal is having enough money to retire. The first step toward making any investment plan is to consider your current age, your likely retirement age, and the *time horizon* between those two points. Even a short horizon is a beautiful thing because it means that there is time to build your savings with investments before retirement. The longer your horizon is, the more spectacular your results will be for those sunset years. If you are 18 to 35 years of age now and you already are earning income in excess of expenses, with low or no debt, the money you set aside in tax-free retirement accounts is better than burying a pot of gold. Way better. CNN Money worked out the following scenarios for its report on "retirement basics":

> Say you start at age 25, and put aside $3,000 a year in a tax-deferred retirement account for 10 years—and then you stop saving—completely. By the time you reach 65, your $30,000 investment will have grown to more than $338,000 (assuming a 7% annual return), even though you didn't contribute a dime beyond age 35.
>
> Now let's say you put off saving until you turn 35, and then save $3,000 a year for 30 years. By the time you reach 65, you will have set aside $90,000 of your own money, but it will grow to only about $303,000, assuming the same 7% annual return.[2]

Because of the power of compounding, the money you save in your retirement account will generate investment earnings, and those earnings will also generate earnings, and so on. It is a wonderful snowball effect.

Are you hearing this loud and clear? The advice on starting a tax-free account is the same, no matter what age you are. If you wish that you had started yesterday, start today. If you wish that you had started 10 years ago, or 20, or 30, start today. With other types of investments, such as mutual funds and individual purchases of stocks, you should also play the longest game you can. The long game is the right play, especially for younger folks, who are—barring unforeseen and historic catastrophes no one would want to contemplate—guaranteed to profit "bigly" (to use a presidential phrase) if they don't screw it up (to use a colloquial expression) by pulling the money out too soon (this is literally the only way you will possibly regret your investments).

Millennials and younger people learned not to trust the stock market because they saw the mayhem on Wall Street in 2008–2009, which frightened us all. But anyone who remembers the crash should also remember the tale of Warren Buffett. As global markets were falling, the Berkshire Hathaway chief was the man who ran toward the crisis, invested heavily, and increased a legendary fortune. In September 2008, all these things happened: the Lehman Brothers investment bank filed for bankruptcy, the unemployment rate hit 10 percent, and the U.S. stock market lost $1.2 trillion in a single day (September 29). Buffett himself described the situation as an "economic Pearl Harbor." And he kept on buying stocks.

"Bad news is an investor's best friend. It lets you buy a slice of America's future at a marked-down price," Buffett wrote in an op-ed in the *New York Times* in 2008. "Fears regarding the long-term prosperity of the nation's many sound companies make no sense. These businesses will indeed suffer earnings hiccups, as they always have. But most major companies will be setting new profit records five, 10 and 20 years from now."[3]

Ten years after that disastrous September, Buffett remains an acknowledged genius and a sought-after sage. You know why? He was right. By September 2018, the Standard & Poor's (S&P) 500 Index was up 130 percent from its postcrisis low. Apple and Amazon had grown—*magically!*—to trillion-dollar valuations.

To be clear, I am not suggesting that investments in stock or mutual funds will offer you consistently excellent returns. It is the opposite truth—that markets fluctuate, sometimes abruptly—that makes the long game the surest shot. In 2017, the stock market performed like a champion. Returns rose by 19 percent over the 12-month period. Early in 2018, though, there was a sudden shift, and the market dropped nearly 4 percent twice on different days in the same week. By the end of 2018, the market had been pounded by sell-offs—the Dow Jones Industrial Average had lost 5.6 percent over 2017, the S&P 500 had lost 6.2 percent, and stocks on the Nasdaq lost 4 percent. At the midpoint of 2019, the Dow Jones Industrial Average and the S&P 500 have rebounded from 2018 like two great power forwards.

If you knew in advance when the market was going to fluctuate, you could be a character on *Billions* on Showtime TV, topping your pizza with caviar and collecting Ferraris (and constantly dodging federal authorities, who'd want to know where you got your tips on when to buy or sell). But even in that fictional TV world, unpredictable things happen, and people make or lose fortunes in the blink of an eye. If you want to know how to make gains without risking everything, there is only one proven strategy: *buy and hold*. I am not saying that you have to buy one particular type of stock and never sell it. But you must put your money into stock investments (generally through mutual funds) and stay there—not pull it out when things start looking sketchy. You have to keep your eye on your personal time horizon, and hang in there until the time is right for you. When markets are down, add money if you can; most important, do not take your money out. Just keep a steady eye on the horizon and remember that time is your generous friend.

ALLOCATION

There's a simple formula for allocating your assets for retirement that has made countless millions of investors wealthier than they ever expected to be at retirement. Subtract your age from 100, and the resulting number is the percentage of your portfolio that you allocate to stocks, which are more aggressive and riskier than bonds. Some mutual funds create portfolios for you based on a target-date formula such as this. These target-date funds—also known as *lifecycle*, *dynamic-risk*, or *age-based funds*—allocate portfolio assets to a more conservative position as your target date—usually retirement—approaches.

Chartered financial analyst and investment allocation writer Carolyn Marsh, among other analysts, has observed that professional investors are trending more toward a "125 – Your Age" formula because interest rates are likely to remain low. Marsh writes:

> With today's low interest rates, investors forgo a lot of return when holding too many bonds—so the recommended percentage of stocks has crept upward in portfolios. The professional investment world is trending closer to a rule of "125 – Your Age" in stocks. We can see this in the growing category of target date funds, which are a good proxy for professional allocation thinking.
>
> Indeed, a look at the three largest target date fund providers—Fidelity, Vanguard and T. Rowe Price—shows that they all hold much closer to "125 – Your Age." For example, these three target date funds allocate 90% in stocks for a 30-year-old and about 75–85% in stocks for a 50-year-old.[4]

Every investor also needs to keep an eye trained on the spectrum of investment possibilities. Your ideal mix should include tax-free investments, bonds, and an array of stocks that bear higher risk and potentially higher return. The sad truth is that most Americans are holding too much cash in their portfolios and not enough stocks. This seems especially true for millennials and gen-Xers. The portfolios of these cohorts have great potential. Unfortunately, millennials and gen-Xers appear to be squandering gains because of an aversion to fluctuating returns.

I get it: the 2008 stock market crash was traumatic. It was a financial fiasco for people caught with too many eggs in the stocks basket and without the time to wait for the market's recovery. Considering my experiences at the Securities and Exchange Commission (SEC), you can be sure I want all of us to learn from the recent history of that time and how many banks, regulators, public policymakers, and institutional investors put on the blinders and doubled down on the boom. But everyone should also avoid being foolish because of an unreasonable fear that a crash is going to happen again. In 2014, six years after the failures on Wall Street, a UBS survey reported that the public at large was still very leery of the stock market—and that younger investors were even more wary than their elders. The survey found that typical millennials are keeping about half their portfolios in cash, just 28 percent in stocks, and the remainder in bonds. Older folks were keeping 46 percent in stocks and about 23 percent in cash.[5] These trends appear to be continuing. But this is precisely the opposite way that these trends should be going at any given time. Financial analysts often refer to millennials as "risk intolerant." Is this some type of new allergy to any investment that isn't strictly blue chip? My prescription is to get a stock injection stat, right into those youthful portfolios.

If you as a millennial investor are in a financially fragile period, say, after college graduation with large student loans to pay, I understand adding more caution to your approach. Fund managers such as Robb Arnott and Rick Ferri worry that cash-poor millennials are raiding their retirement funds when they lose or change jobs: "Ferri has proposed a different 'flight path' asset allocation model which would start young investors with a low stock allocation, gradually reach a high cruising speed stock allocation, and then gradually descend. Arnott, too, thinks a lower initial allocation to stocks makes sense."[6]

Under my program, however, young investors are protected because they have a six-month emergency fund under lock and key. In fact, this discussion makes my point quite well, doesn't it?

IF YOU CAN READ, YOU CAN MANAGE YOUR PORTFOLIO

Of course, there is certainly more to it than cutting up your money pie into the proper percentage of bonds and stocks or retirement and nonretirement accounts. *How you* go about creating a robust portfolio is critical too. The basics are not too complex for you to steer your own course or take a strong hand in it (via a mutual fund account). I'm going to make this broad statement: you probably don't need to hire an investment manager until you're at about the half-million-dollar mark in investments. You can set priorities yourself and then rely on mutual funds to implement them. Be hyperfocused on taxes. Remember that how much you wind up paying on stock gains and bond interest depends on what type of account you invest in. So when you establish an investment account that is not a retirement account with a mutual fund company such as Fidelity, Vanguard, T. Rowe Price, or some other well-established company, the earnings on investments in that account are taxable. This means that if you are looking to add to your allocation in bonds using that taxable account, the first thing to look for is access to their tax-free municipal (muni) bond funds.

A muni bond is one that is issued by a local government or a government agency to finance public projects such as roads, bridges, mass-transit facilities, school buildings, infrastructure repair, and the like. These bonds are secured by either the issuing agency or specifically allocated revenues—for example, bridge toll revenues budgeted for bridge repairs. You do not have to pay federal income taxes on the interest you earn on muni bonds (see Section 103 of the Internal Revenue Code). In most states, there is also an exemption from state taxes on muni bonds issued by that state or local governments within that state. You will need to check this out for your particular state, but if you live in one of the more populous states in the Northeast or California or Florida, I can tell you right now that a money manager, such as Fidelity or Vanguard, operates a dedicated municipal bond fund for your state—and interest is not taxed by the state. If your state of residence doesn't have a dedicated municipal bond fund, you can invest in a general munibond fund. These types of funds hold tax-free bonds from various states. Treasury bonds (U.S. government bonds) are another (state and local) tax-free investment to include in your portfolio through your mutual fund account.

Remember, the type of bond fund you buy depends on the account you are using. In your tax-free investing accounts, buy corporate bond funds that invest in the debt of companies. These bonds are not tax favored but have higher returns, so you want them in your tax-free accounts. Muni-bond funds are the opposite. Because their earnings are typically not subject to state or federal taxes, put them in your taxable investing account. They earn lower returns, but that profit is not reduced by taxes, so there's no reason to put these funds in a tax-protected retirement account.

This is an important point: the only way you want to access bonds is through a mutual fund. The reason is that it is very difficult for an individual investor to get access to bond issuances, and the bond markets are less transparent than the stock market. I should remind you here that I enjoyed a bird's-eye view as a former director of investment management with the SEC. The bond market operated with curtains drawn then, and today it remains the least transparent investment arena in America. The stock market, by contrast, is highly transparent. You can log on to your computer or phone any time you choose and buy whatever stocks you like with 100 percent transparency on prices.

STOCK INVESTMENTS

When investing via a mutual fund, you are generally not required to invest a kingly sum. Most mutual funds require an initial investment of between $500 and $3,000 so that you can limit your risks, but you should still educate yourself a bit before investing your hard-earned money. Before allocating money to stocks, your best first move is probably to look at the S&P 500 Index and get to know it a little. This is an index of 500 of the largest U.S. companies listed on the New York Stock Exchange or Nasdaq and selected by the Standard & Poor's Index Committee based on market performance. The S&P 500 Index is a proven gauge of the stock market's general health that you will hear quoted all the time by financial reporters and analysts. Other important indexes include the Dow Jones Industrial Average and the Nasdaq Composite.

As a second step to perusing the stock market, you might want to take a closer look at the Russell 3000 Index and its subset, the Russell 1000 Index. Although you may have never heard of them, you can use their wisdom about the market, which some say is unmatched, by investing through your mutual fund or by purchasing exchange-traded funds (ETFs). The Russell tracks the performance of all publicly traded stocks, grouped together by industry and size of the company, by growth potential and dividend history and other categories. The Dow Index contains only 30 stocks, and the Nasdaq Composite lists more than 3,000 companies. The Russell's information- and data-rich website provides a valuable contribution to the education of a new investor about index funds.

Russell doesn't offer a mutual fund or an ETF, but some mutual funds track its index. For example, you could choose to invest in the Vanguard Russell 1000 ETF or the SPDR Russell 1000 ETF, and your money will go into stocks of the Russell index. Your approach as a newbie should be to look for roughly the same return as the Russell index. The fee you pay to your mutual fund manager means that you will earn slightly less. By contrast, the work and risk you avoid are generally well worth the fee.

For a slightly more liquid version of a standard mutual fund, consider ETFs. The beauty of ETFs, and few people understand this unless they are professional investors, is that mutual funds can be somewhat more expensive than ETFs to purchase (depending on who sells you the mutual fund). ETFs are simply mutual funds that are traded. A mutual fund is redeemable every day based on its price at 4 p.m. Eastern time, but ETFs trade all day long.

Let's say that you want to redeem a mutual fund. When you put in your request, you will typically be paid the next day at the 4 p.m. (Eastern) closing price on the day you redeem. However, fund managers technically have up to seven days to send you the money. ETFs are exactly the same as mutual funds carrying the same portfolio of stocks, *but* you can trade them any time during the day. Think of ETFs as cutting out the distributor. There's an old saying that "most mutual funds are sold, not bought." To illustrate, think about what happens when you invest through your 401(k) plan: you are offered a menu of your employer's choice of funds. Those are basically being sold to you. You will pick one from among the fixed choices. Somebody already sold those to the employer. In many cases, brokers selling you a mutual fund may get paid a fee for doing so, something that doesn't happen with an ETF.

BACK TO TAXES

As I mentioned earlier, while sorting your investment priorities into stocks and bonds, you also want to be thinking about how to minimize your tax burden. The U.S. tax laws are highly complicated, but you want to structure your investments so that you pay the least amount in taxes under the law. There are three basic tax categories for investment accounts: taxable, tax deferred, and tax exempt.

Taxable investment accounts include bank accounts and investment accounts. You are required to pay taxes on what you earn from them each year when you file your income taxes. Tax-deferred accounts "shelter" your investments from taxes as long as the money remains in the account. These include 401(k) plans and traditional IRAs. There are also tax-exempt accounts, such as Roth IRAs, where you add posttax money and do not need to pay taxes on gains, even at withdrawal. Each type of account has benefits and drawbacks, and those need to be juggled according to your personal situation.

The goal here is to strive for what I call *tax efficiency*. This means that you don't use your 401(k) account to choose tax-free investments such as muni bond funds because the 401(k) account is itself tax sheltered. Never buy muni bond funds with your tax-deferred or tax-exempt accounts. Muni bond funds should be part of your taxable investment portfolio because they enjoy the most favored tax treatment there. Let's say that the muni bonds pay interest rates of 4 to 5 percent. If you live in a state that doesn't tax muni bonds, plus the federal exemption, you are in effect earning 8 to 10 percent because of tax avoidance. Federal bonds that are state and local tax free also belong in your taxable investment account.

In contrast, purchase corporate bonds only for your tax-protected retirement accounts because the U.S. government offers no tax benefits for corporate bonds in any way. One of my IRAs is 100 percent corporate bonds. Corporate bonds typically earn 6 to 8 percent, much higher than munis, and in your tax-free account are not hit by taxes. Enjoying these tax-free compounded gains for 50 years delivers a considerably impressive return.

With stocks, the choice is a little more controversial. If you hold stocks for at least a year, you get an advantage because any realized gains (meaning sales) are taxed at a capital gains rate, which is currently 20 percent. This could be a favorable tax rate compared with your income tax rate. Now that income tax rates have come down under the new tax law of 2018, the capital gains safe haven is not as important as it was. You have more tax flexibility to buy stocks for tax-free and taxable accounts. By contrast, loading up stocks with their 12 percent historic returns into your 401(k) or IRA is powerful for you because those gains compound tax free for decades (if you start early). Under this scenario, common stock funds are highly tax efficient.

As I've said, millennials with their emergency fund in place may have more risk tolerance for stocks in their taxable accounts. The bottom line is that stocks work really well in tax-free accounts, but they also work well in taxable accounts because of the lower capital gains tax rate. I recommend getting your muni and corporate bonds invested in your taxable and tax-free accounts, respectively, to reach your bond investment percentage target. Then put the remainder to work in stock funds, whether in taxable or tax-free accounts.

OPTIONS FOR REAL ESTATE INVESTING

If you like real estate, I recommend that you thoroughly explore real estate investment trusts (REITs). Most REITs are "equity" style, meaning that they invest or own income-producing real estate organized into different types of portfolios. The REITs must distribute at least 90 percent of income to shareholders through dividends.

You can get a piece of real estate action without the risk of buying and selling your own properties through a REIT. You invest by buying shares on an exchange or through a mutual fund that specializes in real estate. Easy-peasy. As noted by my friends at the SEC:

> [m]any REITs (whether equity or mortgage) are registered with the SEC and are publicly traded on a stock exchange. These are known as publicly traded REITs. In addition, there are REITs that are registered with the SEC, but are not publicly traded. These are known as non-traded REITs (also known as non-exchange traded REITs). You should understand the risks of the different types of REITs and their strategies before deciding to invest in them.[7]

As I have discussed elsewhere in this book, a home is an investment, too. If you have purchased a home (following my guidance on having an emergency fund and only taking on a mortgage you can afford), you have exposure to real estate. Make sure that you get your stock and bond portfolio built up before you start buying

REIT shares. Buying REITs increases your real estate exposure, and we all need to stay diversified.

Markets and trading began with the ancient Sumerians and have grown and developed throughout human history, creating conditions for economic growth and wealth formation. Anyone who can read, use common sense, and follow the general principles in this chapter will enjoy the benefits of markets over the long term. The Great Recession left scars on many of us, but history is irrefutable: markets move in cycles. Lotteries and sports gambling are wildly popular but far riskier to your financial health than mutual funds, which hold close to $14 trillion of the hard-earned savings of more than 53 million American households.

As you become comfortable with these basics, you'll be ready to build a habit of a lifetime.

Become a Net Worth Warrior!

The best time to repair the roof is when the sun is shining.
—PRESIDENT JOHN F. KENNEDY

There is an old story, probably apocryphal, of a student sitting in on a college lecture about the world's religions and then stopping by the professor's office. The professor was a wonderful and revered teacher of religious studies. "I loved your lecture," the student told him and, as thousands of young people no doubt expressed over the years, continued, "but I just can't get motivated to take one of your courses. It is hard for me to see how these ideas relate to my life." The professor had a knowing twinkle in his eyes as he said with a smile, "Religion tends not to be a young person's game. The world is your oyster right now."

The professor was right, but the student reminds me of how we talk about money today in America. Building net worth for yourself over the long term is seen by too many as a rich person's game or, even worse, an old person's game.

To be sure, certain corners of the media tend to glamorize the wealthy as an unattainable elite while ignoring the millions of people who have saved and invested to build a strong safety net, secure retirement, and enjoyable lifestyle—without making a spectacle of themselves. They contribute to charities, reinvest in their communities, and ensure that their families can withstand economic turmoil. Millions of Americans are these kinds of everyday heroes.

Unfortunately, irresponsible politicians claim that the U.S. system is dead and buried, implying that people of ordinary means cannot succeed. But this is not true. These everyday heroes take the steps to forge financial security for themselves and their families. All it takes is hard work and following the basic rules of this book.

Anyone starting out in his or her financial life, anyone starting a career, anyone going back to a career after being away from the workforce—whether unemployed, raising kids, widowed, or on temporary disability—has the chance to become this kind of hero. To do this, keep growing your personal balance sheet to greater net worth by following the strategies in this book and *sticking to them*. This is what this chapter is about.

I want you to be ready for the next crisis. I want you to be able to withstand the car breaking down. I want you to able to withstand yourself or your child getting sick. I want you to be able to withstand the loss of a job. Things happen. When you have more assets than liabilities, you don't have to worry that everything will be taken away from you if something goes wrong. If you build your own balance sheet, then your destiny is under your control, not somebody else's.

My dad was the king of the one liner. The truth is, he liked to say, when it comes to our existence, no one gets out of here alive. John Lennon famously said life is what happens to you when you are making other plans. Everyone gets dealt some blows. I don't care who you are. In 2018 alone, Tina Turner lost her oldest son at age 59 to suicide. Bode Miller's 19-month-old daughter drowned in a pool. Anthony Bourdain's shocking suicide left his family reeling. You have my wholehearted prayers that you never endure tragedies of this scale, and the odds are they will be rare. But even minor events, such as the flooding of a basement or an injury that keeps you out of work, have financial implications.

BECOME A NET WORTH WARRIOR: THE BENEFITS ARE LEGION

Job Changing

For young people in the first phase of their careers, a positive net worth gives you more opportunities to change jobs and actually take some risks. Many college students are interested in working for a tech startup after they get out of college, but that can be difficult to sustain without a safety net because those jobs often don't pay well until the company grows. When I left a hedge fund to join the SEC, I was able to afford losing so much income because I had paid off all of my debt and had built up my assets. I never thought from a financial standpoint that I would stay at the SEC for five years, but I was fortunate enough to have the flexibility to make that choice. If you don't like being chained to a job, would be interested in taking a "sabbatical" or joining a friend on a leading-edge startup, become a net worth warrior.

Relationships and Marriages

Many authors and experts have documented the importance of financial issues to relationships, particularly marriages and long-term partnerships.[1] Without question, money problems cause many marital conflicts and divorces. But it is really the lack of communication about money that creates the problems—more so than the problems themselves, because everyone has money problems.

That lack of communication revolves around all the things I am talking about—setting goals for retirement, having an emergency fund, saving for college or professional education, and contingency funds for unemployment. Many couples get married or move in together without putting a framework in place for discussing these issues.

Money also plays a huge role in the survival of marriage itself. Marriage rates have dramatically declined since 1950 for men and women, according to "gold standard" U.S. Census data. This has resulted in part because women have greater career opportunities, and many couples tend to wait until they are both on their feet financially with jobs and savings before getting married. Marriages and "family formation" tend to pick up with good economic times.

The Pew Research Center released a report on marriage and Census data in 2017:

> Half of U.S. adults today are married, a share that has remained relatively stable in recent years but is down 9 percentage points over the past quarter century and dramatically different from the peak of 72% in 1960. The decline in the share of married adults can be explained in part by the fact that Americans are marrying later in life these days. . . . But delayed marriage may not explain all of the drop-off. The share of Americans who have never married has been rising steadily in recent decades. At the same time, more adults are living with a partner instead of marrying and raising children outside of marriage.[2]

Scholars have documented how unemployment and underemployment among men in lower-income communities correlate strongly with a "marriage gap" related to income. As noted in a study by the Hamilton Project at the Brookings Institution in 2012, there

> is no silver bullet for closing the marriage gap, but perhaps the most promising approach to improving family outcomes is to focus on the underlying economic contributors to the sea change in marriage and family structure. Investments in education and training would help put Americans back to work in well-paying jobs, promoting economic security that can lead to more and better marriages—and better opportunities for the children of those marriages.[3]

The roaring American economy of late is creating those kinds of opportunities.

Sadly, our education system sometimes seems to be run for the benefit of its employees rather than its students. We need to focus on improving education to make sure that citizens have the skills to tackle jobs in our fast-paced economy. Teaching some of the financial principles in this book in our schools would help students make good financial decisions when they start working.

When it comes to you and your partner (or future partner), you're going to have to have regular and frank conversations to ensure that you have a strong net worth that will enable both of you to enjoy your lives together. Money can rip a marriage apart—don't let it happen to you.

I recommend that you take the following steps with your partner and weave these into your overall stick-to-it blueprint:

- Meet once a month at a minimum to review your progress and pinpoint money problems to address. Make a list and decide who will handle which problems. During this meeting, neither party can play the blame game; this is for problem solving. This must be sacred.

- If you haven't done so, fully discuss the issue of joint versus separate cash and investment accounts. On one end of the spectrum, you can keep separate accounts, and each can contribute a share to your list of mutual expenses. On the other end of the spectrum, you can merge everything with all joint accounts. Then there is the middle, of course, which involves joint accounts but also each having an individual account for discretionary spending for the things each wants to pursue on his or her own. My view is that keeping everything separate is not a great foundation for cooperation. Yes, some people have strong personalities that need to control their own money, and that is a judgment call. But I favor more transparency rather than less for couples when it comes to money. We are wired to have negative, untrustworthy thoughts when there is a lack of transparency, and that can be deadly when it comes to money.

Couples who regularly talk about money are happier in their relationships than those who discuss finances less frequently.[4] What did Captain Renault say in *Casablanca*? "I'm shocked, shocked!"

Improved Time Management

Would you like to have more time for taking a course, playing more golf, traveling, enjoying new TV shows, or going out with your friends? Americans complain about being busy more than any civilization in history, but it is a reality many of us feel. The importance of work as an end in itself is embedded deep in the American psyche and quickly adopted by immigrants and passed down. Being too busy has become a status symbol among many successful people— perhaps something I am also guilty of, if I think about it. According to a study published in the *Advances in Consumer Research*:

> In the present article we argue that busyness and overwork, rather than a leisurely life, have become a status symbol. In contemporary American culture, complaining about being busy and working all the time has become an increasingly widespread phenomenon. . . . Our investigation reveals that positive status inferences in response to long hours of work and lack of leisure time are mediated by the perceptions that busy individuals possess desired human capital characteristics (competence, ambition), leading them to be viewed as scarce and in demand.[5]

Let's focus on the working Americans who don't fly first class. I am not talking about feeling busy if you are spending four hours a day on your Instagram account or watching reruns of college football games on ESPN. I am talking about the commuting-working-dinner-cooking-chores-kids-bills grind. I feel that.

Net worth warriors save time on finances because they run on a cash-positive basis and don't have to give up weeknights sorting out a mess of overdue bills. They save time because their savings and investments are on automatic pilot. If you set up your 401(k) accounts, taxable investment accounts, and discretionary savings accounts with automatic deposits, you will be automatically sweeping money into those accounts and letting them accumulate profits through long-term growth trends. Buy-and-hold works, so you don't have to.

By investing some up-front time to get all your automatic withdrawals wired into your accounts, you only need to check in on your numbers once a year. It doesn't matter how these mutual funds perform over months. It doesn't matter whether the market goes down or up. Ride these investments long term. In addition, mutual funds are transparent and accountable. I was the nation's chief regulator in charge of overseeing mutual and private funds, and I can assure you that the SEC monitors the entire industry and has stiff disclosure requirements in place. In fact, in the years since I left, the SEC has expanded its efforts to make fund disclosure as user friendly and accessible as possible. In April 2018, the SEC published a request for comment as "the first major step" toward improving the investor experience "by updating the design, delivery, and content of fund disclosure for the benefit of individual investors."[6]

When you stick to it, you may develop an interest in stocks and investing as well as the economy overall. If you have met your priority savings goals and want to try more hands-on investing with a small basket of stocks, great! Be sure, however, to know exactly how much you can afford to lose, and never risk any more than that. You should read a variety of sources. I recommend Morningstar independent investment research at www.morningstar.com as a great source for free market information, analysis, and news.

STICKING-WITH-IT STRATEGIES

Considering the wealth of benefits I've just described, who among us wouldn't want to become a net worth warrior? To do so, you need to counter the mental biases that constitute our most resistant adversary. Although spending provides a lot of recurring short-term gratification, our brains are primed to focus on *earning* more than saving. We have to earn before we can save, and in America, we love and praise earning more than saving. We love to talk about people who climb the ladder of success, whereas those who build beautiful safety nets are so rare they make news.

This is the insight of Eve De Rosa, a professor of human development at Cornell University, who coauthored a study on why Americans find saving so hard. "You hear those stories of someone who has modest means, like that secretary that saved millions," De Rosa told Inverse.com. "That's newsworthy! It's news when someone saves! It's like who would do that?"

"It's more than a financial problem of making ends meet," added coauthor Adam Anderson, professor of human development at Cornell University. "Our brains find saving more difficult to attend to. Even without bills to pay, our brains put a thumb on the scales, making it easier for us to earn than to save."[7]

Embedded in this concern is the fact that we encounter very weak social reinforcement for saving behavior from the media and influencers, as opposed to matters of professional achievement: "winning," going on cool vacations, or living in houses that could someday be featured on reality TV.[8]

Building net worth ultimately brings many of its own rewards. Use these tactics to train your brain to change. It's worth it!

- Here's one that is a foundation of this book, so this isn't a surprise. Automate your savings as much as possible—most employers will offer the ability to deposit a percentage of your paycheck in a savings or retirement account. In this way, money is put in savings without you having to think about it, and once the money's there, you're less likely to take it out. As I've written before, we have strong evidence that this increases accumulation of savings.

- Each year, make concrete savings goals, such as paying down credit cards or maxing your emergency fund within a certain period of time. Tell a few friends who will support and hold you accountable. Think "losing weight," and apply it to saving. We know from Weight Watchers that being accountable to peers is very effective. If you haven't done much saving, I encourage you to start small as long as you keep to regular deposits. Save your money into an account where you can't get at it easily (more on this in a moment).

- Prioritize savings when you receive a new influx of cash (salary raise, unexpected bonus, or inheritance). Evidence suggests that we are less likely to save unexpected windfalls. If you get a raise at work, follow your savings priorities in setting aside the new bucks. Maybe finish off funding your emergency fund or start a new savings account for a family vacation.

- We know that future-oriented mindsets are linked with effective savings behavior. Visualize rewarding experiences you want to happen in your future, say, a splashy wedding, watching your kids walk across the stage to graduate college, or enjoying retirement in a beautiful place in the world you love. Seeing such events in your mind's eye can be part of your meditation or prayer time. Relatedly, one study found that people made better savings decisions after viewing digitally aged photos of themselves. And here's a tip from finance expert Alexandra Talty: "[j]ust like a mood board, cut out some pictures of goals and tape them to a fridge or make a Pinterest board. Saving can be just as fun as spending."[9]

- Have a small but enjoyable celebration when you achieve a savings goal.[10] Be careful about undermining your progress by unleashing any compulsive urges you have managed to leave behind you—whether eating, gambling, or spending wildly.

- Sleep on a big purchase. Even after you've thought about the pros and cons of a new car, kitchen redo, or Caribbean vacation and you've decided you can handle the entire cost, take one more night to be sure. This breaks the impulse circuit in the brain. Then make your final decision the next morning.
- Finally, bankers and policymakers should return us to more normal interest rates, which will help raise up a nation of net worth warriors. Prospective savers, whether rich or poor, respond to higher interest rates for their savings. Because we have left the zero interest rates of 2008–2016, banks will be able to offer higher interest rates on savings accounts and encourage participation with prizes, raffles, and other incentives. As Princeton University guru Sheldon Garon wrote in the column I mentioned in the Introduction, "banks tend to drive small savers away by imposing onerous fees and high minimum balances, forcing many to pay even higher fees at check-cashing services."

I don't consider "savings" accounts that are linked to your regular checking account to be savings at all. If you can transfer the money into your checking account to meet a spending need from your cell phone, it's not savings. Banks should offer savings accounts that reboot the concept of passbook savings from my era, when you had to go to the bank window and formally request a withdrawal. You'll save more and eventually become habituated to saving if you have to exert effort or give something up to make a withdrawal. Certificates of deposit (CDs) have this advantage but have offered dreadful interest rates for decades. I love the innovations seen in the financial and nonprofit sectors with lottery-style raffles for savers and opt-out instead of opt-in retirement savings. Let's bring more creative innovations to savings vehicles at the major banks.

I passionately believe that for all of us and our nation as a whole to prosper, for our communities to begin to heal from the terrible but all too familiar partisan rancor and hatred of recent years, to protect the dreams of our children and grandchildren, we must slay the debt monster and reassert our own economic freedom. We need to drive our economy forward with a newly empowered citizenry with its own positive net worth and minimum consumer debt. We need to reverse the dangerous revival of easy-credit mortgages, have more normal interest rates above zero, and encourage every American to save—really save—for that first house. Imagine how feeling economically secure and safe will ease the paranoia and fear that runs rampant among all walks of our citizenry.

I leave you with the words of two people who were experts with them: first, the beloved British author Rudyard Kipling, winner of the Nobel Prize and author of *Captains Courageous, The Jungle Book,* and *Kim:*

> Savings represent much more than mere money value. They are the proof that the saver is worth something in himself. Any fool can waste; any fool can muddle; but it takes something more of a man to save and the more he saves the more of a man he makes of himself. Waste and extravagance unsettle a man's mind for every crisis; thrift, which means some form of self-restraint, steadies it.[11]

And the legendary American salesman, raconteur, and circus promoter P. T. Barnum:

> A penny here, and a dollar there, placed at interest, goes on accumulating, and in this way the desired result is attained. It requires some training, perhaps, to accomplish this economy, but when once used to it, you will find there is more satisfaction in rational saving than in irrational spending."

In Chapter 10, I share some final thoughts on mastering money.

CHAPTER 10

Financial Literacy for All: Let's Teach Our Children

> To fully participate in society today, financial literacy is critical.
> —ANNAMARIA LUSARDI, DENIT TRUST PROFESSOR OF ECONOMICS AND ACCOUNTANCY AT THE GEORGE WASHINGTON SCHOOL OF BUSINESS AND ACADEMIC DIRECTOR OF THE GW GLOBAL FINANCIAL LITERACY EXCELLENCE CENTER

As of 2019, we have a long way to go in combating the financial literacy gap:[1]

- The United States ranks only fourteenth in global financial literacy behind such countries as Singapore and the Czech Republic, according to Standard and Poor's. However, when comparing U.S. financial literacy with that of other advanced economies, we seem to come out around average: about half "of adults in the major advanced economies—Canada, France, Germany, Italy, Japan, the United Kingdom, and the United States—are financially literate," Standard and Poor's finds.[2] It is safe to say that we can be better than average.
- American teenagers rank average among 18 nations surveyed for financial literacy, behind Latvia and just ahead of Russia.
- One in six of our young people lack the financial skills to meet the basic demands of the modern workplace.
- Four in 10 millennials surveyed in 2014 said that they were overwhelmed with debt. More than half said that they were living from paycheck to paycheck.

- More than half of college graduates with student loan debt report that they did not try to estimate how much their student loan payments would be before taking them on, and a similar number say that they would change how they handled their student loan situation if given the chance to consider the issue again.[3]

As was stated in the *2015 Report on National Literacy*:

We know that financial literacy is linked to positive outcomes like wealth accumulation, stock market participation and retirement planning, and to avoiding high-cost alternative financial services like payday lending and auto title loans. Conversely, financial illiteracy in part led to the Great Recession. To minimize the impact of any future financial crisis, Americans must be educated in personal finance. A great place to start is with our students.[4]

A MICRO HISTORY OF FINANCIAL LITERACY

Now that we have a snapshot of the challenge, what makes financial literacy a useful concept? Where did it start, and why did government and the financial industry start promoting it? Why should we care?

Compared with classic academic disciplines, financial literacy is relatively new. The idea of teaching financial concepts in schools dates back to the early twentieth century, whereas formal curricula and standardized disciplines became codified in the latter half of that century.

The formal movement for financial literacy really started with the campaign to teach domestic science, or home economics, that began with women such as Harriet Beecher and Ellen Richards, the first woman to attend the Massachusetts Institute of Technology. It grew to include the Smith-Lever Act in 1914. This law established a system of cooperative extension services, connected to land-grant universities, to provide any American with information about developments in agriculture, home economics, government, leadership, agriculture, economic development, and other skills. The extension services offered coursework on family financial management, coining the term *financial literacy*.

The Smith-Lever Act was the first federal law aimed in part at improving citizens' understanding of financial concepts and monetary planning. In the 1930s, General Motors Chairman Alfred P. Sloan, Jr., started a foundation that sought to create a "nation of economic literates" through a variety of courses and programs. From the 1940s through the 1960s, financial literacy skills were taught (largely to women) in home economics curricula in high schools and colleges, but financial literacy itself wasn't seen as a separate field until much later. "Home ec," as it was known, was a required course for female students. Belying the commonplace myth that home economics was about baking cookies and learning how to sew, women were in fact taught skills for managing money and home-based affairs, many of them complex. It's no accident that in post–World War II U.S. history, adult women not only "kept the hearth" but the family books as well—and kept an eye on spendthrift spouses. Until social advances began to challenge notions of traditional gender roles, women also had to be amateur psychologists to watch the family purse strings without offending the male egos in the house.

In the last three decades, government bodies, financial institutions, philanthropies, and community organizations have all dedicated considerable resources to personal finance education—as we have seen throughout this book. This has included increased attention in academia, efforts by governments to integrate financial concepts into school curricula and library programs, and a growing body of literature aimed at popular audiences.

This field has garnered increased academic attention since the 1990s. During this period, an increasing number of universities have established dedicated academic programs in financial education and increased the number of academic journals publishing research on teaching methods, program effectiveness, and other topics related to financial education.

This academic focus coincides with a spike in financial literacy programs in the 1990s and early 2000s—spurred first by automakers and other lenders taking heat for predatory lending and then swiftly followed by the passage in 2003 of the Financial Literacy and Education Improvement Act, which established a commission to develop a national strategy. "A congressional caucus dedicated to financial literacy formed in 2005, and the National Association of State Boards of Education established its own financial literacy commission by 2006," reported Rachel M. Cohen in the summer 2019 edition of *The American Prospect*. "In early 2008, George W. Bush issued an executive order to create the President's Advisory Council on Financial Literacy, a body that would ultimately recommend expanding and improving financial education for students in kindergarten through high school."[5] The programs came from a variety of sources, most commonly from community organizations, the Cooperative Extension Service (created by the aforementioned 1914 Smith-Lever Act), and local businesses.

Government bodies, including my old employer the U.S. Securities and Exchange Commission (SEC), the Federal Reserve, and the Departments of Treasury and Education, have all prioritized financial education and dedicated considerable resources to education initiatives. The 2008 financial crisis resulted in a renewed push for financial education in the public sector because the crisis showed that many homeowners took out mortgages they could not afford.[6]

WHAT CAN WE DO TO INCREASE FINANCIAL LITERACY?

If you have children at home, find ways to share what you know about finance and saving money. After all, almost all kids are interested in money. Consider these projects:

- Link parental allowances to specific savings goals. Help set up a savings account for your children at an early age. Parents, consider "matching" your children's savings at whatever ratio you choose.
- If children have jobs, set up and manage an individual retirement account (IRA) to make contributions.
- Jointly manage a small stock investing account with Mom, Dad, or a mentor.
- Start an experimental micro business, including a business plan and payroll.
- Have your kids shadow you or a mentor during a major financial activity, such as planning to buy a new home or purchase a new car.

Education from an early age is another big part of the answer, starting in elementary school and continuing through high school. As of 2016, only 20 states required an economics course in high school, and only 17 required a financial literacy course.[7]

Although public education "mandates" typically give me a stress rash, states with mandatory personal finance high school curricula have had measurable success. Researchers at the Federal Reserve found that "young people who are in school after the implementation of a financial education requirement *have higher credit scores and lower relative delinquency than those in control states*" (emphasis added). The credit scores of high school graduates who have taken financial literacy courses increased as more years passed from the initial implementation of the mandate, which "likely reflects teachers' ongoing learning and tailoring of the content and approach so as to be more effective for their students."[8]

Researchers for Discover's Pathway to Financial Success found that kids who take finance courses in high school save and accumulate wealth during their adult lives at a higher rate than those who don't take these courses. Students who have taken a class in personal finance are more likely to engage in saving, budgeting, and investing. According to another academic study conducted in 2001, individuals who had state-mandated financial education in high school had higher reported rates of savings and higher net worth in adulthood.[9]

Many state leaders are investing real energy and political capital into addressing financial literacy. According to Oregon State Treasurer Tobias Read and Indiana State Treasurer Kelly Michell, who coauthored an op-ed for *The Hill* in April 2018, states are concerned about "a growing number of young adults [who] are also turning to alternative financial services such as payday loans and check cashing services because they are easily accessible." In response,

> many state treasurers are working with local banks and credit unions to ensure that all individuals have access to affordable banking services, and to raise awareness about the importance of saving, investing and managing debt. Stronger public-private partnerships can help support new financial literacy programs and promote smart financial decisions.
>
> In Oregon and Indiana, our offices have worked with the private sector to develop tools that help remove barriers to saving money through various programs and free online resources. Our fellow state treasurers in Vermont, Utah, Rhode Island, Massachusetts and Mississippi are doing the same, while additional states have focused on partnering with the private sector to offer online courses that teach basic financial knowledge to students and parents in schools.[10]

These are encouraging developments.

At the national level, the Trump administration has given its blessing to consolidating redundant financial literacy programs to make progress and put an actual dent in the issue while also achieving budget savings. Treasury Secretary Mnuchin has supported the Financial Literacy and Education Commission, inviting high-profile visitors and promoting its work. As with many such commissions in government, we need private citizens to push the effort forward. The administration's efforts are a step in the right direction.

You can access tons of credible, reliable, and useful information for teachers, families, and young people at https://home.treasury .gov/policy-issues/consumer-policy/financial-literacy-and-education -commission. Also check out mymoney.gov, the federal government's website that serves as the one-stop shop for federal financial literacy and education programs, grants, and other information.

It is easy to be overwhelmed by the resources you can find on the internet about this issue. Stick to a few "gold standard" sources. Bank of America's Better Money Habits and the staggeringly popular Khan Academy have partnered on a platform of financial literacy videos, tutorials, interviews, and step-by-step explanations (https://bettermoneyhabits.bankofamerica.com/en/khan-academy -partnership).

I support the work of the Council for Economic Education, and the council has one of the best sites for teacher resources at www .councilforeconed.org/k-12-resources/.

The National Education Association offers a ton of helpful materials for teachers at www.nea.org/tools/lessons/resources-for-teaching -financial-literacy.html.

Finally, the nonprofit TeachFinLit.org has a comprehensive list of all the best resources for families, students, and anyone interested in mastering money at www.teachfinlit.org/new-teachers/.

RECOMMENDATIONS FOR TEACHERS

What else should government and schools do to help teach our children? My research review points out that most experts agree on a number of commonsense ideas, including:

- Improve teacher training and professional development.
- Provide teachers with take-home materials for students.
- Introduce and/or support additional economics, business, and financial literacy curricula in grades K–12.
- Encourage teachers to use apps and digital tools to engage high school students in learning about personal finance.
- Introduce financial literacy topics to standardized tests.

HELPING RETAIL INVESTORS

To be sure, young people aren't any less informed than many of their parents—including millions of investors. During my years at the SEC, we conducted a study on the financial literacy of retail investors, as was required by the Dodd-Frank law. The study drew on a number of sources, including public comments, a study by the Library of Congress on quantitative studies of retail investors, focus groups, and an online survey.

We found that American investors also lack basic financial literacy, which is not a surprising revelation at this point in this book. I make it here because this is an area where the fund management industry can make a difference.

Many investors do not understand basic financial concepts, such as diversification or the differences between stocks and bonds. Nor are they fully aware of investment costs and their impact on investment returns. The Library of Congress review concluded that "low levels of investor literacy have serious implications for the ability of broad segments of the population to retire comfortably, particularly in an age dominated by defined-contribution retirement plans."[11]

At the SEC, we did identify ways to improve the timing, content, and format of disclosures, as well as useful and relevant information for investors to consider when selecting a fund manager or purchasing an investment product. We found that investors prefer to receive investment disclosures before investing rather than after, as occurs with many investment products on the market. We also identified the kinds of information that investors find useful and relevant in helping them make informed investment decisions. This included information about fees, investment objectives, performance, strategy, and risks of an investment product, as well as the professional background, disciplinary history, and conflicts of interest of a financial professional. Investors favor investment disclosures presented in a visual format, using bullets, charts, and graphs.

We found that investors favor *layered disclosure*. This means an approach in which key information is sent or given to the investor and more detailed information is provided online, with a paper copy of the more detailed information sent upon request.

The mutual fund industry and its advisers must ensure that they are educating their investors in the most effective manner when preparing disclosure documents. The industry has made great strides in the usability and navigability of digital information tools. I am convinced that the industry's recent advances in simplifying how fund performance and dynamics are explained to us have played a role in the increased confidence of investors in our capital markets.[12]

POOR RICHARD SAYS...

I'm planning to start a new organization to support research and practices that lift the financial literacy of children and young people. I'd love it if someday the concepts in this book are "old hat" to far more people than is the case today.

Financial peace of mind is far easier to read or talk about than to achieve, but once your habits are formed, you'll find it hard to manage money any other way. You'll notice less stress, better sleep, and possibly more harmony with your partner or spouse. Financial peace of mind is a great boon to your health. Ben Franklin captured Poor Richard's wit and wisdom in Franklin's book *The Way to Wealth*, read by millions over the centuries since its publication in 1758.

As a book author, I can easily relate to the end of Franklin's parable of Poor Richard:

> "Experience keeps a dear school, but fools will learn in no other," as Poor Richard says, and scarce in that; for it is true, "We may give advice, but we cannot give conduct."[13] . . .
>
> Thus the old gentleman ended his harangue. The people heard it, and approved the doctrine, and immediately practiced the contrary, just as if it had been a common sermon; for the auction opened, and they began to buy extravagantly.
>
> I found the good man had thoroughly studied my Almanacs, and digested all I had dropped on those topics during the course of twenty-five years. The frequent mention he made of me must have tired any one else; but my vanity was wonderfully delighted with it, though I was conscious that not a tenth part of the wisdom was my own, which he ascribed to me; but rather the gleanings that I had made of the sense of all ages and nations. However, I resolved to be the better for the echo of it; and, though I had at first determined to buy stuff for a new coat, I went away, resolved to wear my old one a little longer. Reader, if thou wilt do the same, thy profit will be as great as mine.

If you know of any organization interested in addressing these issues in our schools or with young adults in the workforce, please have them contact me. Discounts for book sales can be arranged by contacting me through my website at www.normchamp.com.

Chapter 1

1. John Pelletier, *Is Your State Making the Grade? 2017 National Report Card, on State Efforts to Improve Financial Literacy in High School*. Champlain College Center for Financial Literacy, Burlington, VT, December 2017; "2017 Consumer Financial Literacy Survey," Harris Poll, prepared for the National Foundation for Credit Counseling and the Boeing Employees' Credit Union, December 2017, www.nfcc.org/clientimpact/2017 -financial-literacy-survey/nfcc-annual-survey-reveals-return -higher-household-credit-card-debt-troubling-financial-trends/ (accessed April 18, 2018).

2. Sheldon Garon, "A Savings Account at the Post Office," Global Public Square, CNN.com, January 12, 2012, http://globalpublic square.blogs.cnn.com/2012/01/12/garon-bring-back-postal -savings/ (accessed April 4, 2018).

3. Vincent Felitti, MD, FACPA, Robert F Anda MD, MSB, Dale Nordenberg MDC, et al. "Relationship of Childhood Abuse and Household Dysfunction to Many of the Leading Causes of Death in Adults," *American Journal of Preventive Medicine* 14(4), 245–258 (1998).

Chapter 2

1. Adapted from James B. Twitchell, *Lead Us into Temptation: The Triumph of American Materialism.* Columbia University Press, New York, 1999.

2. Of interest for further reading: *The Science Behind an Impulse Purchase*, BrainFodder.com, https://brainfodder.org/science-of -impulse-purchases/, accessed June 5, 2018; Philip Graves, "Five Reasons We Impulse Buy," *Psychology Today*, March 2013, www.psychologytoday.com/us/blog/consumer-behavior/201303/ five-reasons-we-impulse-buy, accessed June 5,201; interview with David Kepron, "The Shoppers' Brain: What Neuroscience Can Teach Us About Consumer Behavior," credibly.com, www .credibly.com/incredibly/evaluating-capital-needs/shoppers-brain -neuroscience-key-understanding-customer-behavior/ (accessed June 22, 2018).

3. Tibert Verhagen and Willemijn van Dolen, "The Influence of Online Store Beliefs on Consumer Online Impulse Buying," *Information and Management Journal* 48, 320–327 (2011).

4. Phil Harris, "Australia Is a Nation of Spenders," www.ubank .com.au/newsfeed/articles/2017/07/australia-is-a-nation-of -spenders (accessed June 21,2018).

5. Laura Wagner, "'8 CDs for a Penny' Company Files for Bankruptcy," National Public Radio, August 11, 2015, www.npr .org/sections/thetwo-way/2015/08/11/431547925/8-cds-for-a -penny-company-files-for-bankruptcy (accessed July 7, 2018); Annie Zaleski, "Four Columbia House Insiders Explain the Shady Math Behind '8 CDs for a Penny,'" AV Club, https:// music.avclub.com/four-columbia-house-insiders-explain-the -shady-math-beh-1798280580 (accessed July 7, 2018).

6. Laura Wagner, "'8 CDs for a Penny' Company Files for Bankruptcy," National Public Radio, August 11, 2015, www.npr.org/sections/thetwo-way/2015/08/11/431547925/8-cds -for-a-penny-company-files-for-bankruptcy (accessed July 7, 2018).

7. Tony Chen, Ken Fenyo, Sylvia Yang, and Jessica Zhang, "Thinking Inside the Subscription Box: New Research on E-Commerce Consumers," McKinsey & Co. Global Tech online article, February 2018, www.mckinsey.com/industries/high-tech/our-insights/thinking-inside-the-subscription-box-new-research-on-ecommerce-consumers (accessed July 2, 2018).

8. Lori Swanson, Attorney General of Minnesota, "Unordered Merchandise"; read the entire notice at www.ag.state.mn.us/Consumer/Publications/UnorderedMerchandise.asp.

9. Ron Lieber, "Cutting Off Those Recurring Charges You Forgot About," *New York Times*, January 30,2016, www.nytimes.com/2016/01/30/your-money/cutting-off-recurring-charges-the-easy-way.html (accessed July 2, 2018).

10. www.justice.gov/usao-sdny/pr/scott-tucker-sentenced-more-16-years-prison-running-35-billion-unlawful-internet-payday.

Chapter 3

1. New York Federal Reserve Center for Microeconomic Data, "Quarterly Report on Household Debt and Credit," May 2018, February 2019, www.newyorkfed.org/microeconomics/hhdc (accessed August 19, 2018). "Total Household Debt Rises as 2018 Marks the Ninth Year of Annual Growth in New Auto Loans," February 12, 2019, Federal Reserve Bank of New York.

2. Erin El Issa, "2017 American Household Credit Card Debt Study," NerdWallet, www.nerdwallet.com/blog/average-credit-card-debt-household; Chris Kirk, "Five Charts That Show American Families' Debt Crisis," Salon.com, May 12, 2016, www.slate.com/articles/business/the_united_states_of_debt/2016/05/the_rise_of_household_debt_in_the_u_s_in_five_charts.html (accessed August 21 2017).

3. "Total Revolving Debt, Owned and Securitized, Outstanding," FED Economic Data, Federal Reserve Bank, https://fred.stlouisfed.org/series/REVOLSL (accessed August 1, 2018).

4. Wolf Richter, "Auto Loan Delinquency Rates Are Worse Now Than During the Financial Crisis," *Business Insider*, April 2018,

www.businessinsider.com/auto-loan-delinquency-rates-worse
-now-than-during-the-financial-crisis-2018-4 (accessed July 21,
2018).

5. Jeff Rose, "Can You Really Afford That Car?," *MarketWatch*,
January 17, 2018, www.marketwatch.com/story/can-you-really
-afford-that-car-2018-01-17 (accessed July 17, 2018).

6. Andrew Haughwout, Donghoon Lee, Joelle Scally, and Wilbert
van der Klaauw, "Just Released: Auto Lending Keeps Pace as
Delinquencies Mount in the Finance Sector," Liberty Street
Economics, Federal Reserve Bank of New York, November 2017,
http://libertystreeteconomics.newyorkfed.org/2017/11/just
-released-auto-lending-keeps-pace-as-delinquencies-mount
-in-auto-finance-sector.html (accessed June 15, 2018).

7. "Santander to Settle, U.S. Consumer Watchdog Auto Finance
Claims . . . ," Reuters.com, August 29, 2018, www.reuters.com/
article/us-santander-cfpb-settlement/santander-to-settle-u-s
-consumer-watchdog-auto-finance-claims-sources-idUSKCN
1LE2J4 (accessed June 15, 2018).

8. www.bostonglobe.com/business/2017/03/29/santander-pay
-million-settle-auto-loan-securitization-case-healey-says/cSd
Msa6xp9J5FnPhKfddML/story.html.

9. Ryan Felton, "How Subprime Car Loans Are Ruining Lives and
Repeating the Mistakes of the Housing Crisis," Jalopnik.com,
July 21, 2017, https://jalopnik.com/how-subprime-car-loans-are
-ruining-lives-and-repeating-1796893288.

10. www.troweprice.com/corporate/en/press/t--rowe-price--parents
-are-likely-to-pass-down-good-and-bad-fina0.html.

11. To learn more, Investopedia offers a clear explanation of how
these derivatives worked and AIG's role, www.investopedia.com/
articles/economics/09/american-investment-group-aig-bailout.asp.

Chapter 4

1. Clive Crook, "Housebound," *The Atlantic*, December 2007,
www.theatlantic.com/magazine/archive/2007/12/housebound/
306419/ (accessed February 15, 2018).

2. Peter Ferrera, "How the Government Created a Financial Crisis," Forbes.com, www.forbes.com/sites/peterferrara/2011/05/19/ how-the-government-created-a-financial-crisis/#702aae4921fb (accessed February 5, 2018).

3. Lawrence McDonald, with Patrick Robinson, *A Colossal Failure of Common Sense: The Inside Story of the Collapse of Lehman Brothers.* Crown Business, New York, 2009.

4. "A Decade Out from the Mortgage Crisis, Former Homeowners Still Grasp for Stability," Weekend Edition Sunday, National Public Radio, May 22, 2016, www.npr.org/2016/05/22/ 479038232/a-decade-out-from-the-mortgage-crisis-former -homeowners-still-grasp-for-stability (accessed January 4, 2018).

5. Robert Shiller, "How Tales of Flippers Led to a Housing Bubble," *New York Times*, May 18, 2017 (accessed January 7, 2018).

6. "A Decade Out from the Mortgage Crisis, Former Homeowners Still Grasp for Stability," Weekend Edition Sunday, National Public Radio, May 22, 2016, www.npr.org/2016/05/22/ 479038232/a-decade-out-from-the-mortgage-crisis-former -homeowners-still-grasp-for-stability (accessed January 4, 2018).

7. Ibid.

8. The number of subprime mortgages in the state of Maryland had spiked from 12,800 loans in 2000 to 130,000 loans in 2007.

9. John Leland, "Baltimore Finds Subprime Crisis Snags Women," *New York Times*, January 15, 2008, www.nytimes.com/2008/ 01/15/us/15mortgage.html (accessed January 9, 2018).

10. Peter Ferrera, "Bloomberg Hides Government Causes of Financial Crisis," *The Spectator*, January 4, 2012, https://spectator.org/ 36321_attack-iran-ask-congress-declare-war/ (accessed February 16, 2018).

11. Janell Ross, "Foreclosure Crisis Erases Hard-Won Wealth, Dreams, Even in the Center of Black Affluence," *Huffington Post*, January 31, 2012, www.huffingtonpost.com/2012/01/31/ foreclosure-crisis-prince-georges-county_n_1243151.html (accessed January 4, 2018).

12. Robert Shiller, "The Scars of Losing a Home," *New York Times*, May 18, 2008 (accessed January 7, 2018).

13. Debbie Gruenstein Bosian, Peter Smith, and Wei Li, "Collateral Damage: The Spillover Costs of Foreclosures," Center for Responsible Lending, Durham, NC, October 4, 2012, www.responsiblelending.org/mortgage-lending/research-analysis/collateral-damage.html (accessed January 8, 2018.

14. Corbett Daily, "Home Foreclosures in 2010 Top 1 Million for First Time," Reuters.com, January 13, 2011, www.reuters.com/article/us-usa-housing-foreclosures/home-foreclosures-in-2010-top-1-million-for-first-time-idUSTRE70C0YD20110113 (accessed January 7, 2018).

15. Kelsey Ramirez, "Fannie Mae Raises Debt-to-Income Ratio to Further Expand Mortgage Lending," Housingwire.com, June 9, 2017, www.housingwire.com/articles/40382-fannie-mae-raises-debt-to-income-ratio-to-further-expand-mortgage-lending (accessed January 19, 2018).

16. "Pessimism About Prolonged Housing Affordability Crisis Is On the Rise, 2016 How Housing Matters Survey Finds," MacArthur Foundation, June 16, 2016, https://www.macfound.org/press/press-releases/pessimism-about-prolonged-affordable-housing-crisis-rise-2016-how-housing-matters-survey-finds/ (accessed January 20, 2018).

17. Jeffrey Birnbaum and Alan Murray, *Showdown at Gucci Gulch.* Random House, New York, 2010.

18. Pat Jones, "Housing Industry Lobbying Campaign Rankles Some Tax Writers," *Tax Notes* 42:409–410 (1989).

19. Bruce Bartlett, "Tax Reform's 'Third Rail': Mortgage Interest," *NCPR Policy Backgrounder* 139:1 (1996).

20. Christopher Howard, *The Hidden Welfare State: Tax Expenditures and Social Policy in the United States.* Princeton University Press, Princeton, NJ, 1997.

21. Kelly Phillips Erb, "Eleven Reasons Why I Never Want to Own a House Again," Forbes.com, September 27, 2013, www.forbes.com/sites/kellyphillipserb/2013/09/27/11-reasons-why-i-never-want-to-own-a-house-again/#4be3a91542fa (accessed February 9, 2018).

22. Ibid.

23. Felix Salmon, Interview, National Public Radio, April 17, 2010.

24. David Branchflower and Andrew Oswald, "Does High Homeownership Impair the Labor Market?," Working Paper Series, May 2013, https://piie.c.om/publications/wp/wp13-3.pdf (accessed January 5, 2018).

25. IRS language: "If you have a capital gain from the sale of your main home, you may qualify to exclude up to $250,000 of that gain from your income, or up to $500,000 of that gain if you file a joint return with your spouse. . . . In general, to qualify for the Section 121 exclusion, you must meet both the owner-ship test and the use test. You're eligible for the exclusion if you have owned and used your home as your main home for a period aggregating at least two years out of the five years prior to its date of sale. You can meet the ownership and use tests during differ-ent 2-year periods. However, you must meet both tests during the 5-year period ending on the date of the sale. Generally, you're not eligible for the exclusion if you excluded the gain from the sale of another home during the two-year period prior to the sale of your home. Refer to Publication 523 for the complete eligibility requirements, limitations on the exclusion amount, and exceptions to the two-year rule."

26. Joseph Gyourko, "Five Myths About Home Ownership," *Washington Post*, November 15, 2009, www.washingtonpost.com/wp-dyn/content/article/2009/11/13/AR2009111302214.html (accessed January 15, 2018).

Chapter 5

1. "High Stakes Lotteries Pull in Punters by Making It Harder to Win," *The Economist*, January 2016, https://www.economist.com/finance-and-economics/2016/01/16/high-stakes.

2. Chris Isidore, "We Spend Billions on Lottery Tickets…" CNNBusiness, August 24, 2017, https://money.cnn.com/2017/08/24/news/economy/lottery-spending/index.html (accessed May 27, 2019).

3. National Gambling Impact Study Commission, Final Report, "The History of Lottery in the United States," HistoryBuff.com, June 18, 1999.

4. Kathleen M. Joyce, "Public Opinion and The Politics of Gambling," *Journal of Social Issues* 35(3): (1979); included in Christian Reflection: A Series in Faith and Ethics, 2000–2016, www.baylor.edu/ifl/index.php?id=937582 (accessed May 27, 2019).

5. Ibid.

6. State & Local Government Finance Data Query System. http://slfdqs.taxpolicycenter.org/pages.cfm. The Urban Institute-Brookings Institution Tax Policy Center. Data from U.S. Census Bureau, Annual Survey of State and Local Government Finances, Government Finances, Volume 4, and Census of Governments (1977–2015) (accessed October 16, 2017).

7. U.S. Census Data Annual Survey of State Finances 2016; LendEdu.com, "How Much Do Americans Spend on the Lottery?," June 18, 2019.

8. Cook Clotfelter, "On the Economics of State Lotteries," *Journal of Economic Perspectives* 4(4):105–119 (1990), www.jstor.org/stable/1942724 (accessed January 12 2018).

9. Julie Fleming, "State Lotteries: Gambling with the Common Good," Center for Christian Ethics, Baylor University, Waco, TX, 2011. Used by permission.

10. National Gambling Impact Study Commission, Final Report, "The History of Lottery in the United States," HistoryBuff.com, June 18, 1999.

11. www.baylor.edu/content/services/document.php/144583.pdf (accessed January 12, 2018).

12. Ibid.

13. Max Galka, "The Lottery Is a Tax: An Inefficient, Regressive, and Exploitative tax," *Huffington Post*, September 3, 2015, www.huffingtonpost.com/max-galka/the-lottery-is-a-tax-an-i_b_8081192.html (accessed February 22, 2018).

14. Daniel Jones, "Education's Gambling Problem: The Impact of Earmarking Lottery Revenues for Education," Center for Market

and Public Organization, University of Bristol, Bristol, UK, July 2013; Neva Novarro, "Does Earmarking Matter? The Case of State Lottery Profits and Educational Spending," Stanford Institute for Economic Policy Research, Stanford University, Stanford, CA, 2002; and rising lottery revenues are no guarantee of an increase in education spending. According to the Tax Policy Center, when North Carolina's lottery revenue increased by $23 million in 2010, the state's education spending was slashed by $2.3 billion," Amelia Josephson, "The Economics of the Lottery," SmartAsset.com, January 29, 2016.

15. Melissa Kearney, "State Lotteries and Consumer Behavior," Working Paper 9330, National Bureau of Economic Research, Cambridge, MA, 2002.

16. Arthur Brooks, "Powerbull," *Wall Street Journal*, August 27, 2017.

17. Series of reports by Maine's Pine Tree Watch, 2015-2017. The reports can be accessed at https://pinetreewatch.org/lottery -investigation/.

18. Ibid.

19. Jeff Desjardins. "Why the Lottery Is a Regressive Tax on the Nation's Poorest," VisualCapitalist.com, www.visualcapitalist.com/ lottery-regressive-tax-nations-poorest/ (accessed July 29, 2016). Max Galka, "The Lottery Is a Tax, an Inefficient, Regressive, and Exploitative Tax," Metrocosm, http://metrocosm.com.

20. Geoff Williams, "Poor People Spend 9% of Income on Lottery Tickets; Here's Why," AOL.com, www.aol.com/article/2010/ 05/31/poor-people-spend-9-of-income-on-lottery-tickets-heres -why/19494428/?gen=1 (accessed July 28, 2016); Emily Hailsey, Romel Mostafa, and George Loewenstein, "Myopic Risk-Seeking: The Impact of Narrow Decision Bracketing on Lottery Play," *Journal of Risk and Uncertainty* 37(1):57–75 (2008).

21. Email correspondence with author.

Chapter 6

1. Nelson D. Schwartz, "At Carrier, the Factory Trump Saved, Morale Is Through the Floor," *New York Times*, August 8, 2010,

www.nytimes.com/2018/08/10/business/economy/carrier-trump
.-absenteeism-mo (accessed August 22, 2018).

2.   "Current Employment Statistics Highlights," Bureau of Labor
     Statistics. U.S. Department of Labor, Washington, DC,
     December 2018, www.bls.gov/web/empsit/ceshighlights.pdf.
     Steve Goldstein, "U.S. Enjoys Best Manufacturing Jobs Growth
     of the Last 30 Years," MarketWatch.com, January 4, 2019.

3.   "Civilian Labor Force Participation Rate Tables," Economic News
     Release, https://www.bls.gov/charts/employment-situation/
     civilian-labor-force-participation-rate.htm (accessed August 27,
     2019).

4.   Food Resource and Action Center Resource Library, Monthly
     Data on food stamp participation, http://frac.org/research/
     resource-library/snap-monthly-data-2017 (accessed August 27,
     2019).

5.   "Graves Introduces Commonsense Snap Reform Bill," June 26,
     2017 Congressional press release, https://garretgraves.house.gov/
     media-center/press-releases/graves-introduces-com (accessed
     August 22, 2018).

6.   Table V.C5: DI Beneficiaries with Benefits in Current-Payment
     Status at the End of Calendar Years 1960–2095, www.ssa.gov/
     OACT/TR/2017/V_C_prog.html#1056376.

7.   Chana Joffe-Walt, "Unfit for Work: The Startling Rise of
     Disability in America," "Planet Money," National Public Radio,
     http://apps.npr.org/unfit-for-work/.

8.   Dylan Matthews, Vox, "In Defense of Social Security Disability
     Insurance," Vox.com, February 6, 2018, www.vox.com/policy
     -and-politics/2018/2/6/16735966/social-security-disability
     -insurance (accessed August 14, 2018).

9.   Bob Costello, "New Report Says National Shortage of Truck
     Drivers to Reach 50,000 This Year: Industry Needs to Hire
     Roughly 90,000 New Drivers Annually to Meet Demand,"
     American Trucking Association, Arlington, VA, October 20,
     2017, http://progressive1.acs.playstream.com/truckline/
     progressive/ATAs%20Driver%20Shortage%20Report%202017
     .pdf (accessed May 2019).

10. Russell Heimlich, "Baby Boomers Retire," Fact Tank, Pew Research Center, Washington, DC, December 29, 2010, www.pewresearch.org/fact-tank/2010/12/29/baby-boomers-retire/ (accessed May 8,2019), used by permission.

11. U.S. Bureau of Labor Statistics.

12. Max Nessi, "Generation Go! Career Pathways Initiative," Generation Go! Career Pathways Initiative, Redlands, CA, https://patch.com/california/redlands/generation-go-career -pathways-initiative (accessed August 14, 2018).

13. Lisa Intrabartola, "Rutgers 4-H Helps N.J. Youth Develop Leadership and Life Skills: Children Work with University Scientists on Urban Gardening, STEM Exploration and More," Rutgers University News Release, July 19, 2018, https://news .rutgers.edu/rutgers-4-h-helps-nj-youth-develop-leadership-and -life-skills/20180711#.XYkXV0ZKgac (accessed September 2, 2019).

14. Check out these best-selling excellent and groundbreaking guides to career management: *What Color Is Your Parachute*, by Richard Bolles, Ten Speed Press, revised edition 2018; *The Long View*, by Brian Featherstonhaugh, Diversion Books, 2016; *The New Rules of Work*, by Alexandra Cavoulacos and Kathryn Minshew, Crown 2017; *Fire Your Boss*, by Stephen Pollan (HarperBusiness, 2009).

15. Society for Human Resources Management, *Employee Job Satisfaction and Engagement: Revitalizing a Changing Workforce*, Alexandria, VA, 2016, www.shrm.org/hr-today/trends-and -forecasting/research-and-surveys/Documents/2016-Employee -Job-Satisfaction-and-Engagement-Report.pdf (accessed August 2, 2018).

16. "Employment Is Vital for Maintaining Good Mental Health," Mental Health Foundation blog, June 29, 2012; also, Joyce Modini, Christensen Mykletun, Mitchell Bryant, and SB Harvey, "The Mental Health Benefits of Employment: Results of a Systematic Meta-Review," *Australia's Psychiatry*, August 2016.

17. "Policy Basics: Top Ten Facts about Social Security," Center on Budget and Policy Priorities, Washington, DC, www.cbpp.org/

research/social-security/policy-basics-top-ten-facts-about- Social Security (accessed August 22, 2018).

18. Ibid.

Chapter 7

1. "Left Behind: The Long-Term Unemployed Struggle in an Improving Economy," Work Trends Survey, John J. Heldrich Center for Workforce Development, Rutgers, the State University of New Jersey, 2014.

2. "The Economic Well-Being of U.S. Households," Board of Governors of the Federal Reserve of the United States, Washington, DC, May 2018, www.federalreserve.gov/publications/files/2017 -report-economic-well-being-us-households-201805.pdf (accessed July and August 2018).

3. "Average U.S. Savings Account Balance 2019: A Demographic Breakdown," ValuePenguin.com, https://www.valuepenguin.com/ banking/average-savings-account-balance (accessed August 28, 2019).

4. "The Employment Situation, July 2018," Jobs Report, Bureau of Labor Statistics, Washington, DC, August 22, 2018, www.bls.gov/ news.release/empsit.nr0.htm.

5. "The Economic Well-Being of U.S. Households," Board of Governors of the Federal Reserve of the United States, Washington, DC, May 2018, www.federalreserve.gov/publications/files/2017 -report-economic-well-being-us-households-201805.pdf (accessed July 7, 2018).

6. Vera Gibbons, "Eliminating Credit Card Debt," Real Simple.com, www.realsimple.com/work-life/money/eliminate-credit-card-debt (accessed August 1, 2018); Zach Friedman, "Five Ways to Pay Off Credit Card Debt Faster," Forbes.com, May 21, 2018, www.forbes .com/sites/zackfriedman/2018/05/21/pay-off-credit-card-debt -faster/#79076fa56ebe (accessed August 1, 2018).

7. Remi Trudel, "The Best Strategy for Paying Off Credit Card Debt," *Harvard Business Review* online (hbr.org), December 27,

2016. https://hbr.org/2016/12/research-the-best-strategy-for -paying-off-credit-card-debt (accessed August 24, 2018).

8. "Table 2. Retirement Benefits,March, 2016," Bureau of Labor Statistics, Washington, DC, www.bls.gov/ncs/ebs/benefits/2016/ ownership/civilian/table02a.pdf (accessed August 23, 2018).

9. Alex Goldberg, "Key 401(k) Statistics: Retirement Plans for the Numbers," ForUsAll 401(k) blog, October 29, 2017.

10. Lisa Greenwald, Craig Copeland, Jack VanDerhei, March 21, 2017, "The 2017 Retirement Confidence Survey" www.ebri.org/ pdf/briefspdf/EBRI_IB_431_RCS.21Mar17.pdf.

11. Edward Wolf, New York University, New York; Maury Gittleman, U.S. Bureau of Labor Statistics, Washington, DC; "Inheritances and the Distribution of Wealth; or Whatever Happened to the Great Inheritance Boom?," U.S. Bureau of Labor Statistics Working Paper 445, Washington, DC, February 2011.

12. Alessandro Martinello, "The Effect of Unexpected Inheritances on Wealth Accumulation: Precautionary Savings or Liquidity Constraints?" working paper, September 2016; Knut Wicksell, Center for Financial Studies, Lund University, Lund, Sweden.

13. Cliff Goldstein, "Five Ways to Talk to Your Parents about Their Retirement Income," Marketwatch.com, May 7, 2015, www.marketwatch.com/story/5-ways-to-talk-to-parents-about -their-retirement-income-2015-04-17 (accessed July 9, 2018).

14. Jeanne Eaglesham, "Private Pension Product, Sold by Felon, Wipes Investors Out: Investors Accuse Future Income Payments of Taking Them for More Than $100 Million," *Wall Street Journal*, July 23, 2018, (accessed August 23, 2018); Mark Pugsley, Utah Securities Fraud blog, http://rqn.com/blog/utahsecuritiesfraud/ 2018/07/23/another-scam-comes-to-light-future-income-payments -or-fip/#.W3iKpOhKhPY (accessed August 23, 2018).

15. "Affinity Fraud: How to Avoid Investment Scams That Target Group," October 9, 2013, www.sec.gov/investor/pubs/affinity.htm (accessed August 25, 2018).

16. Ibid.

Chapter 8

1. https://financialengines.com/education-center/employer_match
   _results/.
2. "Ultimate Guide to Retirement," CNNMoney.com, https://money.
   cnn.com/retirement/guide/basics_basics.moneymag/index.htm.
3. Warren Buffet, "Buy American. I Am." *New York Times*, October
   16, 2008.
4. Carolyn March, "Two Rules of Asset Allocation You Need to
   Follow at Any Age," Forbes.com, April 23, 2015, www.forbes.com/
   sites/greatspeculations/2015/04/23/two-rules-of-asset-allocation-to
   -follow-at-any-age/#1bb9ddf05ea8 (accessed September 2018).
5. UBS Investor Watch, "Think You Know the Next Gen Investor?,"
   http://view.ceros.com/ubs/iw1q14-think-you-know-the-next
   -gen-investor/p/1 (accessed September 9, 2018).
6. www.sec.gov/fast-answers/answersreitshtm.html (accessed
   September 22, 2018).
7. Janet Novack, "Target Date Funds Are Setting Up Millenials
   for a Stock Market Shock," Forbes.com, December 19, 2014,
   www.forbes.com/sites/janetnovack/2014/12/19/target-date-funds
   -are-setting-up-millennials-for-a-stock-market-shock-and-some
   -dont-even-know-it/#12a2105c1785.

Chapter 9

1. Just a sample of the many articles and studies out there:
   Patrick Ishizuka, Cornell Population Center, "The Economic
   Foundations of Cohabiting Couples' Union Transitions,"
   Demography, 55(2), 535–557, April 2018; Cheryl Munk, "Separate
   Finances Can Be a Lot Trickier for Couples in Retirement," *Wall
   Street Journal*, June 10, 2018, https://www.wsj.com/articles/
   separate-finances-can-be-a-lot-trickier-for-couples-in-retirement
   -1528683332 (accessed August 28, 2019); Cheryl Munk, "Why
   Couples Should See a Financial Advisor Before They Get
   Married," *Wall Street Journal*, November 1, 2017, https://
   www.wsj.com/articles/why-couples-should-see-a-financial-adviser

-before-they-get-married-1509546214 (accessed August 28, 2019); Stephen Little, "Money Worries Biggest Reason for Marriages Ending," *Independent*, January 8, 2018, https://www.independent.co.uk/news/business/news/money-marriage-end-divorce-day-relationships-personal-finances-slater-gordon-a8147921.html (accessed August 28, 2019); Mary Hunt, *Debt-Proof Your Marriage*, Revell Books, Ada, MI 2004; Dori Zinn, "Why Do So Many Marriages End in Divorce? Too Little of Two Things: Cash and Communication," Debt.com, March 16, 2017, https://www.debt.com/author/dzinn/(accessed September 2018); Michael Greenstone and Adam Lunney, "Marriage Gap: The Impact of Economic and Technological Change on Marriage Rates," Hamilton Project at the Brookings Institution, February 2012, www.brookings.edu/blog/jobs/2012/02/03/the-marriage-gap-the-impact-of-economic-and-technological-change-on-marriage-rates/ (accessed September 8, 2018).

2. Kim Parker and Renee Stepler, "As U.S. Marriage Rate Hovers at 50%, Education Gap in Marital Status Widens," Pew Research Center, September 2017, www.pewresearch.org/fact-tank/2017/09/14/as-u-s-marriage-rate-hovers-at-50-education-gap-in-marital-status-widens/ (accessed September 2018).

3. Michael Greenstone and Adam Lunney, " Marriage Gap: The Impact of Economic and Technological Change on Marriage Rates," Hamilton Project at the Brookings Institution, February 2012, www.brookings.edu/blog/jobs/2012/02/03/the-marriage-gap-the-impact-of-economic-and-technological-change-on-marriage-rates/ (accessed September 2018).

4. "An Ameriprise Study aond Couples and Money," Ameriprise Financial Survey conducted June–July 2016. "Financial Statistics," Money Habitudes, June 12, 2018, www.moneyhabitudes.com/financial-statistics/ (accessed September 9, 2018).

5. Silvia Bellezza, Anat Keinan, and Neeru Paharia, "Conspicuous Consumption of Time: When Busyness and Lack of Leisure Time Become a Status Symbol," in June Cotte and Stacy Wood (eds.), *Advances in Consumer Research*, 42, Association for Consumer Research, Duluth, MN, 2014, pp. 17–21.

6. www.sec.gov/news/press-release/2018-103.

7. Kesong Hu, "Differential Temporal Salience of Earning and Saving," Nature Communications, July 20, 2018, www.nature.com/articles/s41467-018-05201-9 (accessed August 28, 2019). "Neuroscientists Explain Why Your Brain Makes Saving So Damn Hard," Inverse.com, July 28, 2018, https://www.inverse.com/article/47524-how-to-save-money-according-to-neuroscience (accessed August 28, 2019); "Slacking on Your Savings? Cognitive Biases Could Be to Blame," www.eurekalert.org/pub_releases/2018-07/cu-soy072318.php(accessed August 28, 2019).

8. Check out this description of the reality show "House Hunters": "prospective buyers, renters, and real estate agents [as they] go through the home-buying process. *Often dealing with customers who want huge, fully-upgraded homes on a shoestring budget*, these driven Realtors often have to scramble to meet their picky clients' demands" (emphasis added), www.thoughtco.com/buying-or-selling-a-home-top-reality-shows-2875059 (accessed August 28, 2019).

9. Alexandra Talty, "The Psychology Behind Saving in the 21st Century," Forbes.com, May 29, 2015, www.forbes.com/sites/alexandratalty/2015/05/29/millennial-the-psychological-behind-saving-in-the-21st-century/#2df5ac03756d (accessed September 12, 2018).

10. Sheldon Garon, CNN, "A Saving Account at the Post Office," January 12, 2002, http://globalpublicsquare.blogs.cnn.com/2012/01/12/garon-bring-back-postal-savings/ (accessed June 2, 2018).

11. "At a Meeting on War Aims, Folkestone," February 15, 1918, www.kiplingsociety.co.uk/rg_speeches_32.htm.

Chapter 10

1. Research from the Council for Economic Education was essential to this chapter overall; I am grateful for their leadership in this area.

2. Leora Klapper, Annamaria Lusardi, and Peter van Oudheusden, *Financial Literacy Around the World: Insights from the Standard &*

Poor's Ratings Services Global Financial Literacy Survey, McGraw-Hill Financial, New York, 2015, http://media.mhfi.com/documents/2015- Finlit_paper_17_F3_SINGLES.pdf (accessed September 24, 2018).

3. Ibid; "Students' Financial Literacy in a Global Context: The Results of PISA's First Financial Literacy Assessment OECD. Country Note—United States," in *PISA 2012 Results: Students and Money: Financial Literacy Skills for the 21st Century,* volume VI, Programme for International Student Assessment (PISA), Paris, France, July 2014, www.oecd.org/unitedstates/PISA-2012-results-finlitusa.pdf (accessed September 24, 2018); "2014 Wells Fargo Millennial Study," Wells Fargo, June 2014, www08.wellsfargomedia.com/assets/pdf/commercial/retirement-employeebenefits/perspectives/2014-millennial-study-report.pdf (accessed September 24, 2018); Carlo de Bassa Scheresberg Lusardi and Noemi Oggero, "Student Loan Debt in the US: An Analysis of the 2015 NFCS Data," Global Financial Literacy Excellence Center, November 2016, http://gflec.org/wp-content/uploads/2016/11/GFLEC-Brief-Student-loandebt.pdf (accessed September 22, 2018).

4. www.champlain.edu/centers-of-experience/center-for-financial-literacy/report-national-high-school-financial-literacy.

5. Rachel M. Cohen, "As Consumer Protections Dwindle, Schools Push Financial Literacy," The American Prospect, Summer 2019, https://prospect.org/article/consumer-protections-dwindle-schools-push-financial-literacy (accessed August 29, 2019).

6. Bartholomae Fox and Lee, "Building the Case for Financial Education," *Journal of Consumer Affairs,* 2005, 39(1):195–214, March 2005, https://takechargetoday.arizona.edu/system/files/Fox.pdf (accessed September 24, 2018); Tahira Hira, "Personal Finance: Past, Present, and Future," Networks Financial Institute Policy Brief, 2009, www2.indstate.edu/business/NFI/leadership/briefs/2009-PB-10_Hira.pdf (accessed September 24, 2018); John Morton, "The Interdependence of Economic and Personal Finance Education" Social Education, *Social Education,* 69, no. 2, March 1, 2005, https://go.galegroup.com/ps/i.do?p=AONE&sw

=w&u=googlescholar&v=2.1&it=r&id=GALE%7CA130724824
&sid=classroomWidget&asid=f58923b6 (accessed September 23,
2018.

7. "At last count, only 20 states require students to take a high
school economics course to graduate, and only 17 require a course
in financial literacy (Council for Economic Education's 2016
Survey of the States). However, years of substantive and carefully
designed research show that (1) K-12 students can learn economic
and financial concepts when taught by teachers who know economics and know how to teach it, and (2) students exposed to
economic and financial education are more likely to display positive financial behaviors," Council for Economic Education, New
York, 2016.

8. Carly Urban, Maximilian Schmeiser, J. Michael Collins, and
Alexandra Brown, "State Financial Education Mandates: It's All
in the Implementation," FINRA Investor Education Foundation,
Washington, DC, 2015, https://files.ctctcdn.com/e5db0b81101/
f5b36cd4-69bd-4f05-b539- cf73a91c2d73.pdf (accessed
September 21, 2018).

9. B. Douglas Bernheim, Daniel M. Garrett, and Dean M. Maki,
"Education and Saving: The Long-Term Effects of High School
Financial Curriculum Mandates on Adult Financial Decision-
Making," *Journal of Public Economics* 80(3):435–465, 2001.

10. Tobias Michell and Kelly Read, "Improving Financial Literacy
for Future Generations," *The Hill*, April 2018, https://thehill.com/
blogs/congress-blog/politics/384663-improving-financial-literacy
-for-future-generations (accessed August 28, 2019).

11. Federal Research Division, Library of Congress, "Financial
Literacy Among Retail Investors in the United States," December
30, 2011.

12. Visit www.sec.gov/news/press-release/2012-2012-172htm for more
information on the reports.

13. Benjamin Franklin, *The Way to Wealth*, originally published in
1758.

Norm Champ is a senior partner in the Investment Funds Group at Kirkland & Ellis LLP and the former director of the Division of Investment Management at the U.S. Securities and Exchange Commission (SEC). Under his leadership, the SEC restructured many of its operations and adopted a new rule to reform money market mutual funds.

Champ has been a lecturer on investment management law at Harvard Law School since 2008.

Champ's previous book, published in 2017, is titled *Going Public: My Adventures Inside the SEC and How to Prevent the Next Devastating Crisis.* The book chronicles his experiences at the agency and how they shed light on the regulatory process and government policy making.

Before joining the SEC, Champ was executive vice president and general counsel of Chilton Investment Company, an investment adviser to long/short equity hedge funds and managed accounts. Prior to joining Chilton, Champ was at the law firm of Davis Polk & Wardwell. After law school, Champ clerked for the Honorable Charles S. Haight Jr. of the U.S. District Court for the Southern District of New York.

Champ has an AB, summa cum laude, in history from Princeton University; an MA in war studies from King's College London, where he was a Fulbright Scholar; and a JD, cum laude, from Harvard Law School.